T0114524

The Layman's Petition

P. Young

www.trafford.com
North America & international
toll-free: 1 888 232 4444 (USA & Canada)
fax: 812 355 4082

Contents

The Layman's Petition/Preface 2017 US Federal Election

In February 2017 the author of The Layman's Petition (Copyright 2002) contacted a lawyer who had publically indicated a concern with the shifting political environment in both the USA and Canada. In their brief discussion, the lawyer recommended two titles of pertinent interest: EMPIRE OF ILLUSION—*THE END OF LITERACY AND THE TRIUMPH OF SPECTACLE* by Chris Hedges and THE BETTER ANGELS OF OUR NATURE—*WHY VIOLENCE HAS DECLINED* by Steven Pinker. Inspired by these two diverse books and a lifelong interest in social/political issues, the author of The Layman's Petition wrote to the lawyer providing the following context in relation to his own earlier work:

"...Given the US President's 2017 electoral success, a lot of people are asking 'does this help or does this hurt me'? People are expressing surprise at the election's outcome and are examining their thinking with regard to how consciously society is—or is not governing itself. I was caught off guard myself. Has the US President's 2017 electoral success underscored the imperative for a human context beyond the Universal Declaration of Human Rights?

I have not done anything with The Layman's Petition for years owing to the fact that its what-is-thought theme seemed to remain a mystery to the general public and its social equivalency tone apparently too great an affront for civilized discussion. In society, so long as one's livelihood feels secure, there is of course no appetite for uncomfortable questions which might impact the illusion of that security (EMPIRE OF ILLUSION). Everything is viewed through the hardwired and culturally conditioned reactionary filter of 'does this help or does this hurt me'. The question, 'does this help or does this hurt me' naturally depends on a clear and accurate understanding of who and what you think you are, which in turn naturally depends on a clear and accurate understanding of what 'thought itself' is. If you do not have a clear and accurate understanding of who and what you think you are (what thought is), then how can you know what actually 'helps' and what actually 'hurts you'—and therefore then what is the outcome and nature of our subsequent unknowing actions, if we do not know who and what we are (what thought is). How, more to today's unsettling political point, does one participate productively in a democratic election, if one does not know who and what one actually is (...if one does not actually know what thought is).

We seem to have forgotten or never really understood why we require individuals to reach a certain age before becoming eligible to vote. The objective must relate to the concept of an adult as opposed to the concept of a child—the realization that policies and legislation must originate from a larger view of society than the initial/subjective and oversimplified desires of a chronologically conditioned and socially inexperienced individual (child/adolescent). In The Layman's Petition, I am trying to point out that our defining policy statements, (Universal Declaration of Human Rights etc.) are flawed in their failure to define what an 'adult' human being is—what a "Universal" adult human being is. What we have inadvertently done, in the absence of that, is to enshrine the rights of what is essentially a childhood perspective into international law and therefore into the publics' palette of general, oversimplified and short sighted expectations at large. Given the recent US federal election, and that the question 'does this help or does this hurt me' just got a lot more pertinent to a lot more people, I have been encouraged to make another attempt to publish The Layman's Petition.

Getting specifically back to your recommended reads of EMPIRE OF ILLUSION and THE BETTER ANGELS OF OUR NATURE, both books were fascinating and challenging exercises. EMPIRE

OF ILLUSION for spotlighting the electronic/digital divorce from literature (nuance) and its chilling prediction of the developing social/political climate. And THE BETTER ANGELS OF OUR NATURE for the extraordinary and monumental perspective on just how far mankind has actually come in the struggle to achieve peace. I can say that both books were life changing in regard to the discouraged resignation of my thoughts in recent years. I am however a little logistically concerned with Steven Pinker's (THE BETTER ANGELS ...) message that the "Long Peace" is due in part to global trade. Although I agree with many fundamental aspects of that, I am not quite sure what he is ultimately suggesting. A corporate mentality could easily interpret or construe his meaning to be that we can and have 'shopped our way to peace,' and therefore it could follow that anyone who stands in the way of 'shopping' (either free trade or protectionism) would be an 'enemy of peace' ('peace' currently amounting to a global corporate control of markets without constitutional regard for human, environmental or planetary consequences). Mr. Pinker does not really address how mankind would reconcile growing bipolar beliefs about shopping with the fact of finite resources, ecological damage and conflicting age, economic and culture-related interpretations of what human existence ultimately means.

As far as I can recall and I will re-read 'BETTER ANGELS,' Steven Pinker does little to significantly further the articulation—from either a neuroscience or practical consequential perspective—of what 'thought itself' actually 'is,' and so therefore how our consequently unknowing/unthinking (unconscious) markets would police those human and environmental impacts on this 'transition to peace through shopping' (my words). He does address the subject through a discussion about sympathy verses empathy, but he does not, in my opinion, connect an understanding of what 'thought actually is'—with a natural and spontaneous expression of a global adulthood that holistically embraces sympathy (intelligence) without the time-depleting contingent sequential knowledge of specified kinship (expanding circle of empathy). He does indeed spend a great deal of time examining which parts of the brain are active in various neurological scenarios; survival/natural-selection issues, and seemingly hundreds of remarkable observations about the motives, historical context and conditioned interactions of our thoughts; but he still does not, in my opinion, examine <u>directly what 'thought' is</u>. Perhaps Steven Pinker discusses this in his other books, but I am concerned here, in this specific and potentially volatile context, that he is proposing a social/economic scenario that I believe will ultimately feed into existing and future conflicts if it is not tied inherently to a larger discussion about 'thought itself' (and thought's conspicuous absence of a social/legal definition). As we teach adolescents what their reproductive systems are and how they work, so also should we be teaching them what their 'thought' is, and how their 'thought' works. Not what they 'should or should not think,' but what their brain is 'actually doing,' as it builds up the subjective and conflicting complexities of thought, one compounding/conditioned image at a time. As we teach them how to understand their developing sexuality and so prevent unplanned reproductive outcomes, so also should we be teaching them how to understand and recognize their thought's material and chronological parameters, and so enable them to intelligently recognize how and when they are forming physically and philosophically conflicting images about their developing global adulthood.

In The Layman's Petition, my view is that academic society has inattentively perpetuated an auto-verifying lie of omission effectively obstructing the world's population from reaching a timely and spontaneous global adulthood. I do not expect the average person, with their basic consumer/market driven education (legal?)—clinging desperately to the precarious social and financial symbols of that conditioning—to have the energy or opportunity to enthusiastically entertain such unsupported questions. But if one considers oneself to possess a higher education, to be a creator or sustainer of society, then I expect him or her to understand immediately (and profoundly) what thought is and what its full ramifications are.

In Article <u>18</u> of the Universal Declaration of Human Rights, "<u>thought</u>" (the irrefutable fact of it) is the primary (hence first to be stated) issue; followed by its <u>subsidiary</u> issues of: "conscience," "religion" and "belief"—followed in turn by their <u>subsidiary</u> issues of what amount essentially to individual self-expression. Because we have not 'identified' what 'thought' (subsidiary belief) actually is, and because we have consequently and conversely guaranteed the unqualified protection of 'unidentified thought' (subsidiary belief) into law—we have effectively validated and intrusively established the finite chronological/philosophical particulars of one's 'personal entry tradition' (childhood/sequential conditionings) into the context and territory of universal adulthood. We have legislatively and therefore systemically obstructed both the primary acknowledgement and practical development of our own collective global adulthood.

Ask anyone you meet, "What is thought?" and you will see how and why Article <u>18</u> refers to the normal and natural developmental perspective of a child and not that of a fully realized and neurologically conscious contemporary adult human being. 'Belief' (subsidiary of thought) in and of itself, taken as an authoritative and universally guaranteed personal right—and the 'honor' and 'dignity' that therein follows ('honor' as discussed by Steven Pinker)—is really the luxury of childhood and a perfectly logical/forgivable adult imperative of earlier historic times (my words). I 'believe' that most human beings today understand 'belief' to be a *'practical working premise in the absence of larger factual information or perspectives'*. We can still celebrate and respect the sincerity, innocent thought and unimaginable human costs of each others 'entry traditions,' but that is what they are—sincerity and innocence by virtue of their time/ place thought-generated aspirations for a better world. They exist inseparably together—in the context of a universal 'grappling with thought' found in every human entry tradition (spiritual or material)—as viewed through our contemporary insight into 'thought itself' (global adulthood).

In 'BETTER ANGELS,' as a working demonstration, Steven Pinker refers to the Christian Bible as essentially a wiki, a work of many writers over an extended time. He also speaks about the many biblical references to violence as a normal course of action in those periods in which they were written. He goes on to point out that virtually no one today embraces those entries (involving violence) as acceptable, and that the bible, today, is really more like a talisman (pages 11,12 'BETTER ANGELS') than an actual guide/verbatim to daily living (my adaptation of his words). In the same way, most people recognize that "belief" (thought's remedial accommodation of not knowing) without the moderating insight of its conditioned nature, is in fact the definition and recipe for conflict and extremism in all forms. *"...Economy is war by other means."* If one is going to take excessive personal comfort and legitimacy in one's personal entry tradition—to the exclusion of another's—then one must likewise expect to be excessively, personally, and legitimately 'excluded' by that other.

I 'believe' that most human beings today have already moved beyond Article 18 (Universal Declaration of Human Rights) with its vulnerability and obviously divisive consequences and have recognized that as modern adults, we are not "free," to "think," to "believe," whatever we want—but are bound by our collective adult humanity to grasp our true global relationship to each other and our larger sustaining environment. I am not talking about a legislative end to 'developmental belief,' (innocents/unconscious sequential development), just a corresponding legal and realistic treatment of what 'thought actually is'—what a global adult human being actually is. If it is legally acceptable to describe the one (luxury of childhood/

forgivable adult imperative of earlier historic times)—then it is likewise legally acceptable to describe the other (as viewed through our contemporary/physical insight into thought itself/global adulthood).

Article 19 of the Universal Declaration of Human Rights allows us (in fact implores us) to challenge the inherent/strategic neurological ambiguity of Article 18.

I say "inherent/strategic neurological ambiguity," because among many other things: "...*The need for an assertion of 'universal' human rights had 'become evident' during the Nuremberg Trials of 1945-46, when some lawyers had argued that Nazis could be prosecuted only for the portion of the genocides they committed in occupied countries like Poland. What they did in their own territory, according to the 'earlier way of thinking,' was none of anyone else's business."* (Page 258, BETTER ANGELS OF OUR NATURE) (My quotations/underlines)

To proceed with timely, unprecedented and globally legitimate prosecutions, an injunctive functional benchmark in human behavior had to set—Article 18—with the delicate, respectful and universally validating language concerning 'thought itself' to be realized later through Article 19.

It was toward this end that The Layman's Petition was written."
Paul Young, author: The Layman's Petition, April 24, 2017

So here then, with an acknowledgement of its many compositional challenges, is The Layman's Petition as previously presented (©Copyright 2002, 2007, 2010).

(The author does not question or challenge the necessary and strategic mechanism behind the social/political expedient of the individual's inalienable rights, only the neurological ambiguity of it.)

"The significant problems we have cannot be solved at the same level of thinking with which we created them."

Albert Einstein

"The highest that we can attain to is not Knowledge, but a Sympathy with Intelligence."

H. D. Thoreau   *Excursions*

"Intelligence is not personal, is not the outcome of argument, belief, opinion or reason. Intelligence comes into being when the brain discovers its fallibility, when it discovers what it is capable of, and what it is not."

J.Krishnamurti   *The Awakening Of Intelligence.*

The Separation

Father loved the Jazz music and Big Bands of his generation. He was never foolish enough to tell me about it, then he died. He had been ill nearly two years. I had chosen to keep the fact of his failing health to myself. Beyond a single close friend at school, I never knew if the other kids were aware of it.

Father was himself very much a young man, confined to his room, dying from a fatal condition of that dreaded illness. I do not think that my family expected to see him dressed or downstairs again, though it had never actually been discussed. All that remained was to wait out the inevitable. We functioned like a mechanical automation or some sort of silent hypothetical family as the only security we knew crumbled in a kind of numb fear. At school, the contrasting reality of events created a detachment that viewed the day with a cold objectivity. The innocent and carefree antics of my schoolmates provided a sort of strange diversionary distraction. I viewed them as a scientist views a new discovery. I soon realized that the moments of spontaneous camaraderie and clowning around were over because the wall of growing introspection between myself and them was now insurmountable.

I had always made the trip home for lunch, preferring the bike ride and its relative silence to the noise at school. Upon arrival at home I would get the kettle boiling while I made a sandwich and then set the tea brewing. During his worst periods of illness father would be upstairs in bed, but I would not go up to see him until I had his cup ready. There was never any discussion during these brief moments. Father was never a man for idle talk, preferring only to speak if there was a humorous side to something or an improvement of efficiencies

1

that ought to be striven for. He had never died before, and I had never had a father who was dying. So for a man of few words and a boy of fifteen, there was nothing we could say. I would bring him his tea, leave it by his side and then go. We never made lasting eye contact during that phase. Once, I heard him painfully making his way to the washroom but it was time for me to be heading back to school. Not knowing what else to do, I left. I was certain that he still wanted me to keep bringing the tea because he had not indicated otherwise. Perhaps he hoped we would speak, but we never did. Probably it was I who had looked away that single second too soon.

Long before his illness had set in, I had become a problem on the horizon, school was not going well. It was a situation which I knew would not be tolerated especially as my brother and sister were both "straight A" students. An unavoidable confrontation had been building but was then quietly allowed to slip aside as the severity of his illness sank in. I had expected a terrible storm but watched in silence as he began setting like the autumn sun.

Father was one of those men who taught by example, and he took the example even further, leaving you to decide the nature of any discernable lesson. He never let you off the hook by explaining something so finite or pre-emptive as a motive. He was meticulous, a machinist, concerned with both the purpose and the material, detail, and beyond that, the ability of a thing or its main design feature to prove true no matter what the passage of time. He never started or took on a project that he did not intend to finish and a project was not finished until it was absolutely finished. Being a man of very few words, he communicated primarily through subtle shifts in expression. It was like living inside some sort of high-stakes game '... *Guess the Meaning of Life!'* There were no clues, only that almost imperceptible warmer/cooler of his quiet exterior.

There had been times when he could be quite animated, as when we sat together in the yard resting from the exertion of turning the soil in a vegetable patch. Being myself very young at the time, he did all of the spadework while I toiled at the removal of a root, which I had discovered threatening the integrity of the whole operation. As we rested silently on a swing chair which he had reconditioned from an unrecognizable pile of rust, an old man came walking down the street. This caught my interest because there were few opportunities at our previous address in the country, to observe people, other than as they went zooming by in their cars. I knew it was impolite to stare and did not want to annoy my father, so I oriented my head to a point well ahead of the elderly man and strained my eyes to look sideways at the interesting character as he moved slowly past the front of our house toward the lake. I guess my father noticed the misaligned yet corresponding movement of my head, preceding the elderly man as he made his way down the street, and a quick adjustment of his own position revealed the entire scheme. I expected a look of the strongest reprimand if not the actual verbalization of the crime. I prepared for a lecture but to my surprise, he began laughing. Eventually I realized that he was pleased with the situation. Pleased that there had been something going on in my brain and pleased that I had had the attention span to devise a strategy to pursue it. He laughed about it more as he played the amusing event over and over in his mind, engaging me in such a way as to communicate that we were celebrating something together and not was I in any way being made fun of. We went back to our jobs. He quietly cultivating the soil and I tackling the root, a different person than I was only moments ago, having discovered this first clue to his mysterious thinking.

The episode in the vegetable patch was an unusual one. Normally communication had been through that subtler warmer/cooler thing but there was yet another reaction which was more an indication of spontaneous shame rather than calculated interaction. With Father, nothing was initiated unless it served at multiple levels. There were no mindless distractions simply to while away the hours. Every activity, had to, in some way, enhance our development as human beings. So you knew that when he said we were going to see or do something, that 'it,' was something he deemed to be important. Occasionally, situations would arise where events beyond his control would expose us to things that he had not intended us to see. Father, was a man who identified profoundly with the vision of his adopted country. For him, our diverse and varied culture was both a privilege and opportunity for the world to nurture its truer relation. He saw our young country as a place where previously separate societies could let go of their destructive thinking and usher in a new era of larger understanding. Science, in and of itself, was still holding out the possibility of reasonable explanations and through this hope, equality and progress toward healthy relationships for all peoples seemed within grasp. If on these outings an event occurred which flew in the face of that vision, you could feel his sense of almost instant personal shame. He viewed his responsibility to his children, and the world, in such a way that any injustice or inequality was as much his fault as it was the fault of another. He never externalized blame to a source outside of himself and so if in the company of his children, there was evidence of ignorance in the world, then it was to his absolute shame alone.

These 'other instances' were quite rare as he was very good at selecting suitable activities or events for us to attend. It was not as if he was seeking to insulate us from the real world but rather to 'uncover it gradually,' like any parent, as the appropriate values or tools were sufficiently in place. A memorable occurrence of this shameful sort took place one day when the family had gone to see some Native Ceremonial Dancers, at what was probably part of our country's centennial celebrations. There were going to be displays and demonstrations set up in the local park and father had indicated that we would attend, so we all knew it was one of those things he deemed significant. I remember nothing of the day except this single incident. We were crowded around a raised stage upon which the Native Dancers were performing. They moved in a large circle in unison to the beating of a drum. They seemed to me at the time to be very old, though of course I was very young. Their faces and clothing seemed to be worn, tired and weathered but the decorative part of their regalia seemed bright and new and filled with hope. The demonstration continued and by the attention my father gave it, I knew that we were witnessing something extremely important. Father was always insistent that we be aware of all other cultures. He did not explain why but simply continued exhibiting a consistent respect for the evolving historical need in all peoples. The dancers continued around the stage in time to the rising crescendo of drums, an integral part of any young person's developing consciousness, then, somebody threw a single penny onto the platform's hard wooden surface! I could feel my father cringe as he stood slightly behind and to the right of me. A number of the not-quite-so-old dancers continued over top of the still spinning piece of currency proudly ignoring its presence. Then, one who probably was among the oldest, spotted where it came to rest as his motion brought his gaze to bear. He froze in his steps and bent over to retrieve the penny which his weathered fingers could not free from the stage. The other dancers piled up in a growing crowd behind him as he fumbled with the coin, at last physically compelling him to abandon the piece of currency and resume the rotation. The beating of the drum continued. The dancers re-established their spacing and it was almost as if nothing had happened. But it had. Because my father had that uncomfortable expression which said, '...*that was not what I wanted you to see.*'

Years later the bell rang and we poured out of our classes and into the hallways. I had settled into the relentless grind of watching my two separate lives play out; the one at school where I never discussed my father's illness, and the other at home, where I also never discussed my father's illness. I did not resent or fret that the subject was avoided. How else could father or any of us deal with the situation? He had no intention of succumbing to any illness and he dealt with it by proceeding as if nothing unusual was occurring. He endured the surgeries and developing treatments of the day as if they were mere inconveniences. He intended to prevail, so it would have been cruel and selfish to speculate otherwise.

The day was like any other except that the end was now undeniably near. Father was confined almost entirely to bed recovering from a last round of desperate surgical and radiation treatments. He was too weak to join us at the dinner table and only our mother went into their room to tend to him. I still brought him tea at lunch times, during the week, because he would not hear of our mother missing time off work to watch over him. Hour after merciless hour, day after merciless day, week after merciless week, he endured this trial as the disease slowly overtook him. Report cards had been sent home the week before. It never occurred to me that he could or would concern himself with this detail.

As we flooded out of art class and merged with the sea of students travelling the central hallway, I could make out the form of our principal talking to a well-dressed man, outside the main office. I never gave it a second thought from that distance; it was unlikely to be a concern of mine. But as the cluster of students I walked with drew closer, I had the sudden and irrational fear that this man our principal spoke with was my father. There was something about the man's posture, which was deeply familiar, but this could not be possible and so the flush of fear began to subside. I tried to pick up the thread of my schoolmates' chatter as we walked along but could not focus owing to the unsettling likeness of this man's profile to my father. As we closed the final distance, I was nearly paralysed with both shock and fear. The man our principal spoke with, was indeed my father. The motion of the group I walked with carried me forward and as they noticed my consuming concern with this man and the principal, they fell away on either side leaving me to deal with whatever the crisis was. My father and the principal, sensing the direct but hesitant approach of a student, turned to look, and the three of us found ourselves confronting each other face to face. I was completely disoriented, as was the principal. Judging from the grave expression he wore, he had just been asked by a dying parent to watch over a troubled student's progress in the approaching and fatal absence. My father seemed also to have been caught off guard. Either he had intended to slip away without my knowing of his visit or he was not through consulting with the top official. We stood there, the three of us, in an awkward and prolonged silence, scrambling to anticipate the position that each might take up.

I could make no sense of the scene. As far as I knew my father was at home, near death, where I silently brought him tea each day. Yet here he was, standing now before me, like some ghostly apparition completely out of sync with reality. Somehow he had summoned up the courage and physical strength to rise from his bed, shower, shave, dress, drive his manual shift car, which he had not driven for nearly a year, walk from the parking lot into the school and stand there discussing my academic future as if this was just one of any number of completely normal days. I was dumbfounded. Perhaps he was not sick at all. Perhaps the whole thing had been a grotesque and cruel nightmare. But there he stood, with my report card in his hand, clean white shirt, tie, hair neatly combed, shoes still shiny, suit or sports jacket I do not remember, but true to his immaculate form in every detail. Father always dressed this way when there was any sort of function, no matter how insignificant. This was not out of any pretence of class or vanity but because his respect for people and civilised interaction was that high. He never presented himself to us or the public without having first bathed and donned a fresh set of clothes.

He stood there like a living statue, his composed and dignified form still of this mortal world, his disciplined courage pushing the exhausted mind and body beyond the endurable, aware as I was, that this was in fact the first time we had really looked into each other's eyes. Everything had changed. Nearly two years had passed in the ordeal of his illness. I looked back at him now through the eyes of a young adult coming to grips with his own troubled reality. As he held my report card in his hand, it was clear that he was here to see about my grades. Stunned at his presence, but comprehending a change in the equation, I asked him *"What's the problem?" "Your marks!"* he said, *"– They're not good enough!"* I was reeling from the unexpected shock of confronting my two separate solitudes and the sudden and very public scrutiny of my academic performance by the two most powerful men in my life. I did not bodily experience myself to speak it so much as I bore witness to those words that took shape. *"…What difference does it make?"* The principal, realising the tragic gravity of the situation, took a slow respectful step back. He knew that he could not leave because a parent in dire need had requested his presence; wisely, he realised that there was nothing he could say or do to ease our dreadful moment. The situation would of course not normally have arisen, where a father and son would be forced to reckon, immediately, with the undeniable truth of each other's primary reality. Yet here we were, an entire lifetime of interaction being forced into this single exchange, under the threat of looming mortality, and being played out in front of the entire student body as they flowed quietly by on either side of us. *"It matters!"* he said.

There was a long and dreadful silence. We both knew that as each of us spoke in turn, that doors would begin to slam shut. Time had escaped our grasp to these last few seconds of innocence and we both realised that we were about to have our very first and last adult discussion. For that single and only moment, I saw fear in my father's face. He knew that all effective opportunity had run out and that the problems were too large and complex to be solved in the fleeting days that he had left to live. The reality was very much that no amount of extra effort on anybody's part was going to close the widening gap between my failing grades and my brother and sister's "straight A's". We were all powerless to do anything significant about it. My brother and sister could process the disconnected logic of a purely academic curriculum, as it was presented to them. They could remember specific groups or pieces of abstract information and come up with the 'curricular answers' teachers were looking for. But my thought process was different and we all knew it. I had already made my peace with 'general labour' as the order of my life and I intended to see if I could not yet live a dignified life through such means. When he did not speak, in a moment that defies all description, I pressed him: *"...Tell me **how** it makes a difference!"*

Father was silent, despair sweeping away the past and very earth from under his feet. With the opportunity lost, he suspended the desperate intervention. With conviction gone from his voice, physical pain, and what looked to be the purest human isolation behind his eyes, he said, *"...It matters!"* With one simple question – I had destroyed him. Both as a man and a father – just as surely as the disease that ravaged his body. The encounter was over. I left him standing in the hall with the principal. I have no recollection of what could honestly be called 'innocent thought' beyond that day. The very first adult interaction of my life had gone horribly wrong. When I returned home that afternoon Father lay silently beyond his closed door. No mention of the confrontation ever reached my ear. A few short weeks later, Mother helped him quietly down the stairs and into the car. They drove slowly off together, completely alone, past all the familiar sights. I do not know if he was able or inclined to look back at his home. A further two weeks later, only hours after my brother, sister and I had stood silently by his hospital bed, Father uttered his first direct words to my mother about his health.

"...I have finished." For a brief and merciful twenty minutes, my mother and father held each other certain in the mutual knowledge that they must now part. Thirty minutes later, mother called to tell us *"...He has gone."* Together, Father and I had pushed each other to the edge of what superficially defines the individual. There was a flaw in this careless and irresponsible application of human thought and there would be no opportunity for redress.

The Habit of Silence

A [1]lee shore protected by a bluff on a windy day is a dangerous thing. You have to know what it is you are dealing with. As many will tell you, one does not just stumble down to such a shore, launch one's vessel, and then set off as though things were as they appear. A lee shore protected by a bluff on a windy day is also a beautiful thing. It is the one place where a body of water can rest at ease and laugh at the sky with a clear advantage, yet with a moment's inattention or an unsuspecting innocence, it is the one place where conditions can only get worse. Millions of tonnes of atmosphere, perhaps a mile thick, slide across the earth at will then tumble from the crest to stir up the sea and race unimpeded to the horizon. Depending on the height of the particular bluff and the speed of the particular wind, you will always get a wedge-shaped pocket of relatively calm air and a narrow ribbon of undisturbed water following the shoreline. But it is, only a narrow ribbon of undisturbed water following the shoreline.

Like many youngsters, my first job was a paper route and the first twenty dollars of those earnings played at my imagination. Since the age of seven I had been scouring the nearby rocky beaches, below the modest cliffs, searching for anything that caught my eye. From the very tip of the western seawall of a Great Lakes harbour to an impassable zone of red shale cliffs in the opposite direction, I had expanded the permissible boundaries set by my parents and at last gained a free run of the entire shore. I knew just about every inch of the area from knee-deep in water to just out of sight of the gardens

---

1   The author uses this term from a land-based point of view

whose owners dwelt above in the houses guarding the view. I knew all the types of stones you were likely to find on that beach. Not by their scientific names or what they were actually made of, but by how they wore in the action of the waves, what colours they were, which ones you could break and what they would smell like when you exposed their pure inner surface to the bright sunny air. I knew that you could never really predict what size or combination of aggregate might be washed up by a storm but I did know that it had something to do with the way in which it once again became calm.

There were man-made artifacts to be searched out – broken bits of coloured glass and china worn smooth at the edges – pipe, wire, nuts, bolts, brass valves and rusty hinges. Once, a perfectly service-able pocketknife turned up there in the sand, right at my feet, as I dug with my toes while a wave receded. There was a place in the shallow water where the shale was exposed and it formed a prospec-tor's pan to sift out the treasures which generations had lost in the sand of a nearby beach. I would scratch about for hours, sometimes in ice-cold water, feet long since numb, plunging my hand into the frigid medium only when I was certain of an item's value or inter-est. There were coins, most of which I had never seen before. Tiny five-cent pieces, silver, with intricate borders of maple leaves. There were dimes and quarters to match and oversized pennies with the same sort of ornamentation but their borders accented with a line of prominently raised dots, which seemed to enchant me. I could see that these coins were of my own country but of a time so seemingly distant that they fascinated me as if they had come from another planet. The 'good ones' went in my left pocket and the contemporary ones in the right and when the shale and the currents would yield no more, it was off to the corner store with soaking feet to spend the surplus on chocolate or candy. Trapped in the cracks and hol-lows of the red shale bottom were thousands of old square nails of every imaginable size – handmade I was told – and mysterious oval and round stampings of solid steel, probably three-eighths to one-half inch in thickness, which were never identified. There were spoons, forks, badges, commemorative pins, clasps, belt-buckles and interesting brass reed-plates from old harmonicas, the melody and ascending scale still suggested in the slots which defined the pitch, each a little shorter than the one preceding. There were similar pieces of brass-work of a different configuration and they were the front and back plates of old clock movements, measuring in their work the very thing that laid them waste and delivered them here to my hand. There were half a dozen gold and silver rings and two little lead figures whose fragile extremities had become detached. I never questioned the presence of these artefacts. They had accumulated as naturally as snow drifts behind an obstruction. They had been lost or discarded by any manner of human misfortune and the action of predominantly shearing waves had carried them to this point where a peculiarity in the shore-line impeded their progress and I bent over, standing in the shallow water, the reflection of a brilliant sky to be overcome and picked them up.

There were natural phenomena to be kept track of, crayfish, insects, mallards and geese. There were smelt in the spring and shiners in midsummer which washed up dead by the thousands. There were suckers and carp and later when artificially introduced, huge salmon. There were great schools of minnows in numbers inconceivable that seemed to stream along the shore and appear like a dark river flowing within the water itself. These graceful migrations of miniature fish, which would oblige you to remain absolutely motionless for a quarter hour, generated frequent and surprising flashes of light, the brilliant overhead sky being captured in their reflective undersides as particular individuals glanced sideways off the bottom to relieve some irritation. There were enormous goldfish said to have been released as smaller ones into the wild and a species of minnow or fry, so tiny, that it could only be seen in the direct sunlight, its translucent body looking like some sort of afterthought as it followed the dark speck of its minute eye through a ridiculous expanse of universe. Sitting perfectly still on a rock one day, there was a sudden rush of noisy and turbulent air. Four huge swans labouring extremely hard to regain altitude had startled more than themselves. At the very end of the street upon which we lived, where the land fell away and that Great Lake began, where that old man would walk to and stand silently looking to the horizon, savouring some memory, there was a cluster of large boulders which thrust out from the shore. There was a main group of them that offered a variety of stepping stone routes toward the deeper water and a larger rock further out than the rest. The further out you went, the fewer were your options but the more secure became your footing. If the water was unusually low, a final set of boulders emerged claiming a few extra feet from the 'sea.' As small children, we balanced jumping back and forth from rock to rock and round about trying to avoid bumping into each other yet remain in motion. The story was that at one time these rocks secured a large deck right on the water and that dances of some sort were once held here. There were strange little bumps or peaks of water that occasionally darted about appearing and disappearing, confounding me for years, until one day I saw where one came ashore, lifting the dried leaves in a fleeting whirlwind and carrying off a milkweed seed until it disappeared from view.

The first twenty dollars from that childhood paper route was bound to be tied up with the lake in some way and as I excitedly described a small boat that a schoolmate had for sale, I failed to notice the look exchanged between my parents. Years before, shortly after I was born, Mother had stood helplessly on this same shore, a baby in each arm and a small child at her side as my father was carried away in a Styrofoam sailboat by a seemingly harmless-looking offshore wind. As he dwindled to a speck on the horizon, she grew frantic with fear. Alone with her young children in this strange new country, she dare not lose sight of him for fear of his vanishing forever, but she had to tear her eyes away in what might be a last mortal glimpse and immediately seek help. At that moment, a vehicle pulled up with a trailer in tow and a group of skilled rescuers began launching a boat as their captain consoled her. An observant resident had seen the whole thing unfolding and had called the authorities. Father was retrieved, the boat was disposed of and now I was describing the purchase of another one exactly like it.

It was twenty-five years before I learned of this story in relation to that childhood purchase-proposal and began piecing it altogether. Mother and Father had simply pretended that they were unconcerned about the impending acquisition and the next day Father had enquired as to whether there were any 'other boats for sale' in my 'price range'. As it happened, there was. Another schoolmate was pushing hard to persuade me to buy his family's canoe which had lost its canvas and so fallen out of use. It was not what I wanted as my heart was set on flying like the wind, but as father had offered to drive me there and see it, I figured it was a step in the right direction. We inspected it topside and underneath and from stem to stern and it was agreed that it was actually in good shape. *"The wood is solid,"* he said, *"– last a lot longer than Styrofoam! Could have a coat of fibreglass, be painted and in the water by next weekend!"* The money was out of my pocket in a flash. The canoe was secured to the roof of the family car and we disappeared in a surprisingly uncharacteristic cloud of dust.

The next weekend, more or less true to his word, he snuck it down to the water's edge to test it out having told me it would be later that day before the paint would dry. He had waited until I was at the farthest reach of my beachcombing to the west and then had hurried it down the embankment and launched it into the water. It was no use though because I had seen the flash of gleaming orange paint as he carried it down the steep bluff and was wildly on the run. I arrived in time to find him soaked to the skin, waist-deep in water, carefully spilling the contents out of the swamped boat in order to re-float it. I was informed, most scientifically, that one *"... should not sit on the seat – as the boat would become unstable."* I was lashed into one of those passenger-issue type life preservers that chafed your neck at every move and then set free with a stern warning to heed the *"offshore winds."* The following day an elderly neighbour called out instructions from the top of the cliff, *"Move up – to the thwart!"* *"Roll your wrists – like this!"* (Going through the exaggerated motions with his hands that would lead one to an insight as to how it was actually done.) *"That's right! Off you go!"* That tiny canoe, with its curved keel-free underside and full beam, had been designed by an infinite number of human interactions with wind and water and so represented an ancient knowledge of the 'real' environment. When coupled with the seemingly endless hours of relaxed exploration, it was and is with its unobtrusive accommodation of almost every relevant condition, perhaps one of man's most remarkable small vessels.

Bobbing about in the waves, being borne up then down by the will of the wind, the wind itself having been born of the weather, the weather of the sun, of the air, land and water, or being silently slipped away sideways as even the faintest breeze prevails at last over one's own greater mass, it was easy to see that everything connected in a single unfolding motion. In the hours of this silent and private communion with nature, free from the classroom's socioeconomic focus and academically prejudiced assertions, where always the suspension of a paddle's will resulted in the resumption of nature's business, I wondered, *"...what was really going on in the mind of man"?* I knew that terrible things had happened in the world. I knew that terrible things were happening and that according to some sources they would go on happening. I knew that here on the beach a heavy object concealed in sand would become exposed if a wave carried off the finer material. I knew that if a large enough wave struck the heavy object, it would itself be borne up for a moment and nudged along a fraction or a foot, as it must, depending on the power and angle of the wind, which struck the water, which struck the heavy object, which shuffled it along this modest stretch of beach. It was easy to see that all things happened in sequence, in relation, one thing following another then in itself setting the conditions that would in turn affect all things that follow. If the world was in a mess, my innocence concluded, then it must be the fault of something that went before.

The reflection of the sky upon the water, sun, brilliant light, clouds, the colour blue, the mesmerising distortion by ripples of images upon and below, I learned by familiarity to see beyond this and when I could not, to manoeuvre the canoe that its sideways inertia swept a window of calm to follow its lee and like the cliff above, gain a momentary glimpse of what lie beneath. At school, they were focussing on the distortion instead of the thing, the reflection, the image, and not the source of the common intelligence or reality which lies beneath and no one seemed consciously or openly concerned about this. I could never 'become something' in the attitude of an 'intellectual choice,' as if life's worth were a grovelling trip to the shopping mall in search of fleeting distractions. It negated the integrity and respect for life, nature and society that my parents were trying to demonstrate. To the shore I would go, and the water, and the reflection of the sky, and with the investment of a little effort would paddle across the shimmering blue and clouds beneath, but it was no illusion of some 'artificially privileged flight,' because I knew it to be only one distorted reflection of a common origin. It became my refuge, my re-connection to a larger reality as the institution my parents valued primed me for and toward accepting failure. Education, as I experienced it, was on a fundamentally and in my view morally and therefore democratically flawed journey, and things like stones, pebbles, wind and waves and one human being connecting to another through the timeless dignity of our simple and life sustaining tasks, did not seem to interest them. Their minds were set on means as if the result could be reaped in some inert isolation. I sympathized with the ageless movement of life around me but froze in a deep personal horror at the shape of a living earned solely through the product of social division.

Years later, on a sharp spring morning, I recklessly sliced the tiny canoe through the quarter-inch ice that had formed overnight, the shattering and splintering shards sliding underneath each other or careening off over the surface as the brittle tension was released. I struck out in a wide arc revelling in the fantastic noise it made compared to the summer's usual fluid silence. As my radii increased the distance from shore, the duration of acoustic sustain set up a roar-like echo from the cliffs. I stopped paddling and was astonished to hear just how long it continued. I played with this effect, stopping and starting until I realized that the sound coming back to me was the same sound reaching the shore. Suddenly, the trees, houses, parked cars and garden sheds seemed to be looking back from shore with decided displeasure, my self-indulgent activity having torn into the quiet morning air. There was not a soul to be seen yet it made you feel a stern disapproval. I floated there, silent, amid the chips of ice as a thin film of freezing water advanced slowly over the dark frozen surface.

There was nothing to be done with any dignity but adjust my course ninety degrees and head directly inshore and skulk silently back along the beach and up the bluff until better conditions prevailed. Resolved in the clear absence of any better options I started boldly for shore but after the briefest succession of powerful strokes, I found myself doubting the wisdom of the noisy dash. Slow progress was out of the question because sufficient forward inertia was critical to a successful penetration of the ice and adequate steerageway, but this noise now seemed destined to bring out the whole town. I floated again, silent, searching the brain for a way to get ashore without the disruptive spectacle. Self-conscious, I contrived a relaxed glance to the horizon behind me then leisurely back along the shore and about the various landmarks of intimate familiarity. Something did not add up or was suspiciously out of place. I retraced the awkward charade ending up at the view astern and the perfectly flat expanse of ice, which from that low angle, appeared to stretch off to the horizon. I could see the trail of shattered crystal that my passage had left behind but the trouble, it turned out, was that the destruction had the appearance of stretching clear to the horizon, with no trace of the ninety-degree turn I had only moments ago made. Viewed from the crest of the modest bluff this band of fresh ice appeared to extend about a half-mile from shore, the rest being clear glittering open water. I had known that a sea-level view was a questionable thing but this illusion was completely unbelievable. Looking back toward the horizon you would swear that a vessel had crossed an enormous body of water skinned over entirely with ice. Not only was the dazzling sparkle of the morning sun on the frigid lake beyond invisible, but so was the evidence of the ninety degree turn I had only moments ago made. It was a startling revelation to learn that my vantage point of some twenty-four inches over the water's surface was so dramatically flawed. I had by this time been paddling extensively for several years and studying the horizon still longer and had never suspected a breach in practical perception of this magnitude. Without even thinking of the disturbance that had only moments ago silenced my paddle, I effected another ninety degree turn and headed off parallel to the distant shore, crunching and smashing my way along in a determined bid to measure the actual phenomena. Father had once said that it was 'twenty miles to the horizon.' After thirty minutes of crashing and thundering and ninety-degree turns, I was confident in concluding that there was considerably less than a thousand feet to mine.

In a moment of plain insanity, I considered standing up in the canoe to change the angle of perspective and perhaps witness the actual instant of visual transition. The thought brought me back to reality and the ridiculous nature of the activity[2]. Stepping out of the canoe on shore and surveying the silent expanse of broken ice, I was impressed to note even this advantage of rising to one's feet. With the canoe and a sense of novel accomplishment balanced easily on my shoulders, I headed up the embankment using yesterday's still frozen footprints. Half-way up the elevation I caught a momentary glimpse of the chaos I had caused below, the seemingly random jumble of broken ice starting to resolve itself into a traceable record of measurement and grid-like deviations. At the crest of the bluff, I set the canoe down to study the patterns I had left behind. There it was, viewed from this advantage of a homeward journey, and even the moderate elevation of expedient thought, a record of the destructive curiosity and experimental consumption that had validated the shape of my every move. I had got-ashore in the guise and justification of self-expression without a scrap of guilt for the disturbance or destruction I had caused.

The beauty and danger of a lee shore is that you have arrived at earth's meditation, the place where some of her biggest differences relate silently and unseen. Enormous bodies of atmosphere slide away invisibly carrying off millions of tonnes of surface water, the cold clear depths welling up to replace them like a spring of unimaginable volume. To the horizon, no matter how high your vantage, the angle must at last become so slight. You see everything yet you see nothing. The pencil-line in the distance conceals the whole of our world and

---

2   Cold water can kill in minutes. The author has never launched a small boat into cold water since this day and does not in any way encourage the activity.

closer at hand the eye reveals only what comes back in contrast. I remember late fall days, the breeze cool, the sun warm, the sky brilliant blue and an ocean-of-air floating away a single cloud born aloft and I, sheltering in the protected warmth below the ridge, absorbing what could only be called a private respite joy.

...Father loved his Jazz music – the small groups and the Big Bands. Each week the whole family clambered onto the couch in front of the television to watch them perform. He kidded with us one evening while watching the show by keeping up a surprisingly pointed inquiry; *"...if you had the chance – what instrument would you like to play?"* He had that unusual playfulness about him, much as he had done that day on the swing chair when we worked in the vegetable garden. By what now was obviously no coincidence, a newsletter came home with me from school the next week. A music program for students in grades seven and eight was being initiated, *'...instruments purchased in bulk could be ordered at a reduced rate'.* Before I knew it I had a gleaming new instrument in its own case and was part of a program to illustrate that music could effectively support a child's education. I followed it through those last two years of public school and on into high school. In fact it became the subject which held out the last thread of academic appeal for me, a kind of last-ditch attempt to hold on to the natural childhood and community relationships that should have followed one easily through a healthy social lifetime. But the socio/academic die had been cast and no one seemed realistically concerned that nearly one third of us were walking away in a very deliberate and self-contained silence.

After Father died, I quit school. The years piled up and I drove most of this socio-academic injury from my thoughts, except that horrible encounter so close to his passing. It is the one constant thread from adolescence etched into the mind that will never fade. It has haunted and shadowed every adult moment of my life that our disagreement over the core value of education should have been so conveniently avoided, to my obvious advantage, by his untimely death. Had he lived, and mother regretfully confirms this, he and I would surely have gone separate ways. Why is it always in life so easy to estrange and in death love? Father has remained there, in thought, every waking moment of my life, pressing back, *"...think it through – finish our conversation!"*

It was easy to shift blame, to find things wrong with the world, to attach responsibility to people or events that had gone before. If the world was in a mess, it was simple to point a finger and say *"that's where it went wrong;" "they should have done this or they shouldn't have done that."* Eventually I left the shelter of my beloved ridge with its prevailing offshore wind and ribbon of calm and I entered a storm pursuing what I considered to be the healing of those previous injuries, developing fantastic logic and arguments to illustrate how my parents' generation had fumbled the ball. It offered the illusion of relief from the sense of obligation to be doing something about the chaotic state of the world. But it never erased the memory of the pain and disappointment and fear on my father's face.

Almost twenty years would pass in the exercise of these evasive strategies before an unusual radio program brought this 'Big Band Sound' flooding back into consciousness. It was a remarkable re-introduction, with a host who was, *'meticulous, concerned with both the purpose and the material, detail, and beyond that, the ability of a thing or its main design feature to prove true no matter what the passage of time.'* It was an attitude of social sincerity and diplomatic resolve from another time. It was an approach I remembered only too well and the encounter was akin to a collision with that dreaded scene in the high school hallway. There was my father, I could see him in the mind's eye, standing just off to my left, and the principal, a step back to the right and in the background, the sound of our soon to be familiar radio host, meandering in an uncannily straight line, by virtue of his seemingly nonchalant word and deliberate programming, saying, *'I want you to listen to this, I want you to listen to this.'*

The three of us, my father, the principal, and I had stood frozen twenty years. We had witnessed the undeniable truth of a blatant socio-academic discrimination at the very core of our parent/child interaction and had for our own immutable reasons remained silent. We were three participatory accessories to an ongoing socioeconomic divorce and alienation of the worst possible kind and had watched the organic innocence of my youth founder on the lottery of society's transient and perverse appetites. Both 'winners' and 'losers,' arbitrarily hewn, by ignorance, from the wood of life's single nourishing root. My father and the principal and I had stood implicated all this time. Not daring to move, not daring to speak, lest the fragile evidence of that truth disintegrate. And here was this radio host, contrasting the miracle of his art-form so sharply against the contemporary guise of that violating and accelerating social/academic indoctrination, splicing observable twentieth-century recordings together, saying in the continuity and silent moment of that wilful and/or unconscious recognition '...*I want you to listen to this, I want you to listen to this...'* And I did listen. And it was as if he had found physically where my father waited and had brought him here to this very moment, and said, *'I want you **both** to listen to this, to that fleeting and fragile silence which precedes this and every act of human recognition.'* I listened and felt my father there, tangibly with me, listening to the same contemporary presentation of those historic melodies, weighing their now undeniable implication, in light of even our own small alienation, and he urging me, over and over, almost with anxious desperation, *'Finish our conversation!'*

Father, you have become astonishingly real. A simple radio program has dissolved almost a quarter century, perhaps even my concept of death itself, and it has put the frail thread of your human aspiration so very clearly within my own grasp. This changes everything. The need to express so explicitly seems to evaporate. We have been attacking through society's vulgar marketplace accusation, the distorted image of our own inner being.

I have been told that you were always a thoughtful man, thinking long and hard before you spoke. And although I have tried all these years, to apply your level of self-discipline to my own thoughts, the effort has yet to bring me one verifiable inch closer to any larger reality of a truer society. But as I know you did in your task so shall I persist in mine. My generation and those on either side must finish this act of rising collectively to our feet and embracing that global responsibility of which your history so painfully and clearly implicates to us. I have tried to be your son, worthy of the hopes and dreams that you held for my future, but also to be true to that clarity of conscience to which you and your generation so proudly aspired. I do not and can never know whether you found a way to forgive this pain I caused you. But I must find with my contemporaries the courage to think out loud and by the result of that thought, to know whether you and I are reconciled, to know whether the generations, nations, and separate personal predispositions, as separate bodies of neurological experience, can ever meet.

You were anxious, if not in words then by implication, that I should finish our conversation, a conversation which cannot occur where this world refuses to acknowledge the vacuum. Society cannot learn from the pivotal and complicating aspect of history it continues to deny. This education, which you placed such importance upon, cannot hope to serve anyone where its direction is mandated by an invented authority whose innocent and naive aim is no more than a childlike auto-verification. Who educates? Who decides what manner of criteria influence our curriculum? Who decides what measure of honesty, is enough? The point of education, surely, would be to dispel ignorance and division, not nurture and replicate the shallow neurological polarization that still threatens to destroy man.

It is time to legislate a little more 'independent thought,' between the 'intention of education' and the self-preserving logical expedient of the spatially defined bureaucratic state that administers it, much in the same way as the higher courts have been empowered as a check or balance somewhat separate from the gross or manifest state. How else are we to discover that self-defeating aspect of our own spontaneous pleasure which so consistently translates into the other's pain? Our constitutions and charters do not actually describe or acknowledge the key vulnerability of the human condition. They are remedial tools merely, intended to prevent us from slipping ever backwards. They cannot hope to free or secure us from the contempt or hatred of others where their very wording defies the source and origin of the fundamental or founding neurological offence. Our charters and constitutions are not comprehensive recipes for liberation, but rather incremental reactions against the ever manifest conflict born out of the oppressive nature of our own ignorance. How are we to achieve a safe environment for anyone, where our underlying need is shaped and identified through a collectively legislated shunning of reality?

Conflict is the cold hard physical fact of unexamined or incomplete thought. It is a material object striking another material object. Thought, in and of itself, has not rid us of this suffering yet we make no effort, either as a society or educating body, to nurture the intelligence to openly discuss this. We are neither educators nor parents who resign ourselves merely to the administrative inertia of a contemporary bigotry. No human being can be measured, described or socialized by a system whose action is the replication of its own spatial/sequential logic; education is about removing barriers, not building them up. A value system is merely a value system – a finite set of assumptions, assertions and self-sustaining measures that spring from the very physics of spatially polarized thought itself. Who is to police our locality oriented neurological behaviour when it is we ourselves who have ignited and validated the very division? Who is to come at the intelligence of this thing if not our global and universal kinship in its totality? Man is not an isolated corporation who sets out to manifest random sequential evidence to support his own path to personal relevance, collecting phenomena and stimuli to decorate and adorn his own particular ego, without lasting repercussion.

What is routinely called education, I identify to be essentially a lie. Consciously, or unconsciously, told to ourselves or each other, a lie by sustained democratic indifference none the less. People died fighting to develop, maintain and defend the world's struggle toward peace, equality and Justice. Shame on each and every one of us who reaches the outward condition of so-called adulthood and who does not step forward in support of advancing those discussions toward a more timely description of the actual global human condition. We are human beings, all of us, capable of feeling both physical and psychological pain. If we continue to live by thought's unexamined spatial expedient, we shall die by thought's unexamined spatial expedient. You have made a statement of values that the strength of your own integrity forces me to deny. The passage of time has left us distant yet it is clearly the very same struggle. The magnitude of history's effort and sacrifice has left us silent, yet silence on this account will serve us not a moment longer.

The Layman's Petition

The central concern in life, that confounds both young and old, is how universally divided man seems to be. Whether it is through belief, culture, economics or generational reference, our individual organic-thinking seems always to become paralysed by one's own particular chronological sequence or sense of personal development. If these personal developmental sequences or experiences are markedly different from another's, growing up in the forties as opposed to the seventies and discussion fails to translate or reconcile that condition, then it seems to become accepted (or adopted) that these individual developmental differences must in some way be profound or insurmountable, and therefore that this ideal, concept, or exaggerated preoccupation with the individual's definition and validation, and therefore the culturally supported subsequent quest for ultimate 'individual fulfilment,' becomes legitimized. Each one of us pushes ahead hoping to achieve personal authoritative proof of where we have been as individuals, rather than looking forward, coherently, to see collectively where we are actually going.

Most people, on the surface, seem to be professing a satisfaction or strategic resignation with the unfolding logic of their socio-economic political/environmental state of affairs. The writer, in this case, freely admits that the apparently logical pursuit of this sequential development, on his part, has led to little else than vulnerability, isolation and the erosion of any larger meaning. I value my relation to life and society, but society, for the most part, does not value its relation to me. This is true at least in part for most of us, at some level, whether we have had the opportunity to realize this or not. So at the global level this pursuit of a purely cumulative concept of personal identity becomes a self-defeating exercise, always attracting the indifference or persecution of one group or another whom we have failed to acknowledge, validate, or respect in the strategic contrivance of our own chronological meaning.

In this lopsided preoccupation with our own fancied personal development, it is, by definition, necessary to abstract self-interest out of the wholeness that sources us. At this same time we are also saying that we want to nurture and instil in our children an appreciation for and of the collective. But the two social/intellectual ideals, in the final analysis, are utterly incompatible. History repeatedly tries to impress upon us that there is no safe-level of sustained or verbally unqualified 'self-interest'. The simplest reconciliation for humankind could stem from the broader social recognition of a neurological cause and effect reaction which effectively negates any validity of the dictionary or statistical concept of 'self.' This largely unconscious cause and effect personal identification could be the primary factor distorting our ability to think, co-operate, or express intelligent adult meaning together.

It has been talked about at length that there was a noticeable turning away from broader social relationships, in our western cultures, following the Second World War. People apparently and I think correctly became suspicious or fearful of things like nationalism, grand ideals or larger visions of exclusive 'social-self,' which so clearly played an inflammatory role in man's vulnerability toward seemingly unavoidable violence. We apparently turned away from these larger divisive/cultural hierarchies and focused our attention on the more regional interests, the simpler pleasures of personal convenience or the enhancement of the particular individual's enjoyment and immediate economic security. The very idea of larger collective contexts, nationalism or universality, seem to have become forbidden subjects suppressed in most quarters as a necessary means to avoid outright confrontation. It seems we have subsequently said to our children, *'Only expression stemming from the uniqueness of the individual is legitimate.'* Out of this deeply isolating yet strategically understandable development, my generation was born.

Although it may be obvious to seniors, it is important for my contemporary predisposition and developmental awareness to distinguish between these two dramatically different social orientations. In the case of your generation there is the appearance of it having been a population born out of, nurtured in, and embraced by a larger social context. But you were, it then appears, forced to de-emphasize or renounce parts of that social context as a necessary and remedial expedient toward maintaining peaceful foreign/domestic relations – all inflammatory or contentious identification with culturally sequential heritage was suspended. My generation, however, was born directly into this measure of what could be called a 'larger social renunciation.' It is not as if we were born with an inherent insight into larger collective contexts and have therefore de-emphasized them due to their innate vulnerabilities. It is not like that at all. We were actually 'born out of' and 'nurtured in' this atmosphere of the individual first and society second. We do not have any formative or referencing experience of multigenerational collective context other than the marketplace evolution of our own immediate group of peers, who have, by immediate proximity, shared the identical or nearly identical experience of contemporary social/sequential development.

Although possessing natural and self-evident social potential, my generation is, at this moment, as you know, profoundly disenfranchised, lacking in any functional ability or realistically nurtured outlet to reflect or relate broadly in a collective multigenerational sense or to relate constructively, as if we had a viable or achievable stake in this fragmenting future. There is no socially defined or politically acknowledged perspective of broadly legitimized human inquiry that we can consider or focus on collectively, and so there is no broad-based deliberate forethought at all. My generation is, despite its panicked stampede toward these global communication technologies, the very personification of a deepening human isolation. We are aware of a thing to be done, a collective role to be played in history. We know that there must be an achievable way to account for all people, all generations, all things and perhaps even account for the frustratingly finite feel of our psychological selves, but it still continues to be proving impossible to reconcile this with the shallow, meaningless and purely economic/consumer footing of our day to day lives. Our very existence has counter-evolved into this infuriating inability to seize what has clearly become history's final and fading moment of truth. The inevitable result is that we are left to cast our eroding 'social currency' with the aggressive and rampant pursuit of this so called 'personal fulfilment,' despite its obvious absence of any larger sustainable organic/social interaction, or, cast our eroding 'social currency,' with those who would through a more naked form of violence, tear down such an inherently flawed social/political/technological assumption. There is apparently no neurological middle ground. There is apparently no place where the common soul can stand up in an act of simple good will and call for some sort of strategic or broadly endorsed time-out.

It must be possible to share a collective and sincere moment of honesty regardless of the factors, accumulated years or visible identities that have shaped and diverged our apparently separate cultures. We lack, it would appear, an agreeable starting point or reference where we can pick up the task of exposing that aspect of our shared consciousness which is suspiciously present at the outset of our recurring vulnerability toward systemic isolation, conflict and social paralysis. *Our past is sequential-development. Thought is a finite sequential process.* In the pressing imperative of the now, the individual's social/sequential-development, thought itself, spawned out of and sustained by memory, manipulates to maintain the pragmatic operational application that it is free from the influence of place or time. *'Thought,' thinks it is beyond 'thought'*. We cling to this personally accumulated appearance of 'neurological identity' as if it were somehow objective, as if it were invulnerable to history, as if it were separate, as if it could establish lasting spatial independence or organic security from the resulting effects of a consistently fragmenting world thought-process.

The whole division is sustained and perpetuated through a sort of treadmill of the moment, a constant impulse to express as if we were the first generation to actually see daylight. It has been an unstoppable force deriving sustenance and inertia through our organic inability to access detailed objective long-range memory, and so our thought is, and has been, impulse, reaction, and all its inherent vulnerabilities to prejudice, fashion and aimless academic achievement. Up until now, collective social thought has had no immediate emotional evidence that it could lay consciousness on, identify with, and say '. . . *All these people were essentially – us! . . . They thought, spoke, aspired, felt joy, sorrow, and finally anguish all through the exact same instrument of consciousness employed this second.'* It is the same neurologically vulnerable brain. Past, present, future.

The whole thing seems to have perpetuated through a static cultural threshold of collective social/neurological inattention, or so it seems until this juncture. But today there is a dawning and remarkable recognition of what it means to have mankind's technologically or mechanically recorded visual image and audio voice. Early light and sound recording devices have left dated and detailed traces of our inescapable kinship with the past. Phonographic recordings and rare film footage have left haunting images of our very own consciousness trapped in the physical rationalisation of eternity. Our folly has been sustained through an absence of admissible evidence to the contrary but sub-sequent generations, through this astonishing imagery, have begun discovering the vulnerable blind spot in the machinery of the unexamined human psyche. Through our parents' and grandparents' spontaneous aspiration, we have begun discovering the crushing and yet time embracing realization that we are achieving absolutely nothing new and that we are, ourselves, the very 'thing' we seek so desperately to escape.

Something fundamental in man's equation has changed with the introduction of sound and picture recording technologies. These early experiments have captured moments and frozen them in undeniable relevance. Some images are kind, joyous, some images cruel and unspeakable, but all images are immune to the moment of threshold's prejudice by the successful leaping of what was once impenetrable time. These recordings in themselves are indifferent to our interests, yet still they are retrievable at the beckon of will. The sequential flow of psychological time has been destroyed. Man turns at last, in the first person, whether young or old, to see himself as he really is.

With the reluctant turning away from those established social/ sequential contexts and the ensuing struggle to find meaning in isolation, society has turned that same flawed eye to rest upon the progressive details of its own collective disintegration. *'What can I do about it'* is the universal self-absolution. It is as if we thought peace could still be purchased by a brinkmanship-like selling off of the future to subsidize a stalled and stalemated social evaluation. We have chosen a systemic and escalating civil erosion over direct conflict in the hope that some form of sanity will magically appear before the tide overwhelms us. With the seemingly unstoppable ap- plication of violent (to violate) foreign/domestic policy, (the linking of Profits to Democracy and therefore of Profits to Justice) and the therefore ensuing planet-wide private/corporate exploitation of the larger human/organic vulnerabilities, many of us are coming to realize that as it stands, there will be no bright socioeconomic or organically sustainable interaction for any of us. We are coming to realize that there will be no available or achievable place or location to actually call home and therefore no peace of mind regarding even the most basic necessities of life. There will be no geopolitical security into any status quo future. In other words, we are coming to realize that there is no 'exploitable sequence' of 'personal development' for us. 'It' has been 'used up' and subsequently transformed into this sarcastic search for irony and situations to amuse or mock the fact of our very existence. We are coming to realize that worst-case scenarios for mankind are now distinct and emerging realities. With the mounting evidence of environmental degradation and the concentration of so called wealth into fewer and fewer hands, all bets for the safe/sustainable future seem to have been quietly slipped aside. Apparently it has become the pre-articulate, income-focused, entrepreneurial hope that modern and ancient societies can still be exploited, to the very end, having never known or experienced the simple universal birthright of a larger collective meaning. 'Security,' sought through the expression of an unexamined belief/self-identity system, sustained and nourished through the 'insecurity' of a broadly unexamined domestic thought process, threatens the entire global/organic manifestation.

People seem always to have been aware of an alternative to this chaos and an apparent characteristic of that same consciousness, which chooses to suspend its fixation on impending calamity and focus on the next achievable step. There surely exists a groundwork for something truly simple, honest and humane woven amongst the silent thought of man's seemingly eternal anxiety. There surely exists in our world, a cross-section of international societies comprised of both young and old, yearning to take an unattached and collectively verifiable look at the divisive nature of our present condition. Now that we have by default rendered the good-life worthless, surely we are at last in some sort of position to reflect broadly.

This music of the Big Band era, with its emerging sense of haunting significance provides an insightful and provocatively strategic contrast to the limited nature of my own particular development. To recognise en masse, that we are, each of us, the result of a spatially unique sequential development, is to recognise en masse, that we are – 'sequential development'! To recognise en masse, that we are 'sequential development,' is to recognise en masse, that we are, at a deeper level, the very same 'consciousness'. We are, each of us, a sweeping timeless undercurrent capable of recognising and equating innocence – any innocence – as unconscious sequential development. It is the echo of the evidence of our universal human being.

We are logically capable of peace, harmony and understanding, but have faltered in a childlike confusion cultivating our separate identities through convenient sequential advantage and inherited good fortune. We have perfected our 'individual selves' to the brink of a most disgraceful indignity. Loved ones have been lost. Time continues the relentless filtering of the unspeakable things that we have done to each other. Opportunities to be naturally honest have been let slip away. I know that you know my generation wastes under the burden of needless and psychologically exhausting counter-identifications. I know that my generation seems powerless to seize the advantage of learning from the pain that you hold in living memory and that if this living memory and implication of pain is lost, then in fact the meaning and lesson of all sacrifice is lost. I know that each day there are fewer and fewer living vessels of this extended memory and that each day it is more and more the responsibility of each adult human being to 'think'.

It has never been history's place to define or dictate how future generations should interpret existence. But history must validate its own sequential relevance to eternity by acknowledging, at a profound level, the necessity of a truly objective and thoughtful human reflection. It is the very proponents of history who must drive this question forward. It is 'history itself' that must set the benchmark. History must acknowledge and be seen to be acknowledging the broader contextual aspiration necessary to contemplate the extraordinary and catastrophic drama that continues to grip man's struggle to know himself. We have all, each of us, each generation and nation in its own way, struggled to have this discussion. But in the absence of any clear or defining parameters for the 'instrument of conscious identity,' the result has degraded into one of almost universal suffering and disaster. Conflict, isolation and a fearful erosion of the human ideal has become the norm.

Through this indulgent ignorance of and about our own thought process, we have unleashed a nightmarish maze of childlike competitions and progressive statistical validations. We have fallen into and perpetuated a quest to prove unilateral affirmative authority where no such thing exists. The chaos lies in the very instrument of thought itself. Reading solely to affirm one's own established position is far far worse than any outright illiteracy. A shallow concept of the self has been sustained and we have remained in this childlike state, caught in the foolhardy lie of it, compounding the neurological mistruths with reckless abandon hoping the display alone will achieve the purely emotional ends. We all want our particular pasts validated, our 'sequences of development' respected, but the sequence of development, in itself, is never the original source of awareness, only the record of memory or survival driven locally through time. It is not evidence of any profound or fundamental knowledge of self nor is it a guarantee that any previously established means of survival, no matter how robust, will continue. Consciousness, as we express it, never precedes or witnesses its own birth, so it is absurd to profess any profound authority, any profound specific individuality, beyond that of simple developmental prejudice or the locally manifested 'entry tradition'. We are struggling to express ourselves solely through the manifestation of a recollected sequence and so are rendering our separately accumulated identities, our 'physical and psychological locations in time,' societally invalid. Our relationship, our global kinship, our love and compassion for each other, must lie in intelligence. It certainly does not lie in any manner of spatial/mechanical or cumulatively opposing thought.

We still fail, even as a supposedly modern and educated society, to discern any significant or socially implicating difference between our 'thought' and our 'intelligence'. As one writer[3] of interest attempts to explain it,

'...*It is not possible to 'think about intelligence'. 'Thought is thought, which in and of itself is not intelligence'.*

We can though, he laboriously points out, '*think about thought, because it is of its own nature'.* He goes on to suggest...*If we 'think about thought,' it will be noticed that the 'activity of thought' abates somewhat and 'consciousness' then defers, in some measure, to the implication of a previously unrecognised depth of relationship...'*

Where there is that kind of consciousness or non-personal intelligence, there might be a capacity to recognise 'self' in every external, implied or implicated thing. It might be possible to suspend this assumed and fearfully self-centred primary significance of chronological location that has so profoundly divided and put man at risk.

There is a growing number among my generation who are discovering the challenge of understanding this troubled world through the emerging context of our parents' spontaneous or contemporary music.

---

3   The author of The Layman's Petition is paraphrasing significant points from his understanding of J. Krishnamurti's book *THE AWAKENING OF INTELLIGENCE.*

Fortunately there are broadcasters with vision who have understood not only the need to serve that demographic who created and evolved this music but also to serve those generations who follow and who must find the backdrop against which to contrast the direction and attitude of the present society we are ourselves creating.

As a younger person, I have been listening to a group of Big Band and Jazz radio programs and reviewing both the music and its manner of presentation at great length. Seniors may find this a surprising or odd development but your contemporary means of self-expression is of course completely unlike anything I previously identified with. Without this very deliberate study, there would not have been a materially logical context through which to recognise the relevance and obvious organic continuity that it offers. My generation, being a product of those post-war wider social renunciations, simply finds it inconceivable to have anything significantly in common with an alternative consciousness not of its own peer group or developmental sequence. Society has, of course, subsequently fragmented into this vast array of diverging social and generational realities. Until I discovered the surprising and unexpected appeal of your music, I had no accessible evidence that it could or should necessarily be any other way. I have been listening thoughtfully to your radio programs and it leaves me troubled. I am troubled because of the gulf between your generation and mine and because of the scope of the critical things that we should have talked about. I am troubled because you seem to be remembering a very specific human significance which you have been unable to visit upon my consciousness. There seem to be countless songs here that suddenly astonish me with their timeless beauty and spontaneous sincerity. Songs like *STAR DUST, BEGIN THE BEGUINE, WONDERFUL WORLD, SERENADE IN BLUE, BEYOND THE SEA, MY PRAYER,* and *BERKELEY SQUARE.* These songs, despite many having emerged from under severe conditions, have a non-confrontational and physically drifting effect that my brain and body know nothing about. They have a romantic sincerity and melodic symmetry that compels the coarser nature of my contemporary thought process to stop. The list of melodies seems endless and comes effortlessly into view through the emerging comprehension of my own impending mortality. I am humbled in ways and as never before. There is a logically affirming relationship, through culture, where I previously thought there was none.

My generation was born of your history's strategic or larger social renunciation. Like my peers, I lived in those finite moments left vacant where separate visions and value systems meticulously avoided each other. I lived in this therapeutic, cultural and historic sterility and struggled to impose some sort of lasting value on it. But it has evolved into and become an obsolete and increasingly dangerous social/political isolation. I want and need the warmth and timeless human companionship suggested by your music, the joy that my generation does not seem to know. But I want, and can only accept it, honestly, with a clear and unbiased understanding of where and why your loved ones were lost amid such unspeakable violence. I want and need a clear and universally verifiable explanation of the cognitive process, which leads to such inexcusable loss of life. This does not mean content, I am not at this point asking about specific events in history. I am asking quite specifically about the 'instrument of thought and consciousness itself,' the 'medium' out of which this history arises. I want a clear and verifiable treatment of legitimate cognitive activity, as it pertains to the adult human being. And I want a clear and verifiable treatment of the dangers of identifying solely with sequence, as it pertains to the dangerous and compounding assumption of the right to unqualified self-expression. Whereas history has not solved conflict through any sub-collective or cumulative thought process, we ask for your blessing to let us seek each other through our underlying intelligence. This is the central desire born out of your post-war social renunciation experiment.

The so-called golden era of popular Jazz and Big Band standards, could quite easily, for modern generations, fit the criteria of a new idea. It is a discovery or evidential example of what it might be like to express conscious meaning beyond the isolation of our inherited spatial/chronological location. Is any one of us to deny this naked truth of a vulnerable generation swept-away by history? Is any one of us to deny the repeating ignorance of our thought, articulated in time, without humility? These melodies, our parents' parents' music, can be our healing phenomena within attainable distance and these affirmations are the very same affirmations which comforted this very brain in so many perishable bodies before us. It could be our ribbon of calm protected by a ridge of permanently recorded memory in this very transient and disposable time. Modern generations must invoke their own gentle and respectful permission to contemplate history's anxiety. We must find the place where our promise of a global heritage went missing. This music of the Big Bands, with its haunting bittersweet sentiment, seems to come from the proximity of the last place where our parents truly smiled. This is the challenging contradiction that confounds and measures our growth to this day.

The Search for a New Lee Shore

At The Ship Builders Memorial, on Georgian Bay, a man stood defining the wisdom of Collingwood's vision to embrace the timeless and I approached him to enjoy that interaction. Given the context and intimate way his hand related to a piece of machinery, and posture to pride, I took him to be a former employee of the local Shipyard. We talked nearly an hour and I learnt that he was in fact a Merchant Marine sailor in World War 2 and that he had gone on to serve thirty years as Chief Engineer on ocean-going vessels. I could scarcely believe my luck and asked him to comment on a steam engine displayed near to where we stood. We examined the piece of machinery and explored the merits of two conflicting explanations of its origin. One thing certain about its past was that this particular engine was used to drive a massive water pump, which would empty the Dry Dock, and its distinctive venting of high-pressure steam from a single-expansion cylinder would signal the wives of many a shipyard worker to return a waiting supper to its oven. The labouring of this engine, which I sadly never heard, was apparently one of many unmistakable rhythms and sounds heard emanating from within the Shipyard operation. Our discussion was rewarding for both of us and proper introductions were in order.

As we walked along the promenade of The Ship Builders Memorial to where my wife sat, I explained that we often came here Saturday or Sunday evenings, if the weather was warm, with a small radio to listen to a Big Band radio program. Frank Sinatra had just started spreading his news as we came within earshot of the softly playing music. My wife and I, born just either side of 1960, were clearly not of the generation normally associated with this music. Our retired Merchant Marine sailor looked back and forth between us and the radio in utter disbelief, *"that's Frank Sinatra!"* he exclaimed, as if it couldn't possibly be true. Something remarkable about the situation had struck him and he was for a moment utterly speechless, finally drawing our attention to the thousands of goose bumps raising the hairs on his still powerful looking arms and hands.

I think about this encounter often because it seems to suggest a profound cultural healing. Suppose for a moment that this Veteran of World War 2 had never heard Sinatra sing, perhaps even until the year I was born. And suppose even further that he had heard only one Sinatra tune every second day of those forty years, which is not at all inconceivable. Then that would still suggest that he had heard old 'Francis Albert' sing about 7,300 times. He could not possibly have experienced that precise emotion on each of those 7,300 occasions or his goose bump reaction would surely have been entirely played out. There must have been something fundamentally human or profoundly satisfying about this situation that made him hear his own period of music regarded as relevant, on this the near side of a long and socially isolating dark age. The heart-rending music of an epic era had survived through the pendulum swing away from that experience and a new generation was making ready the possibility of relating directly and personally to that painful period.

Forty minutes east of The Ship Builder's Memorial on yet another beautiful body of water is the small city of Barrie. There is a Citizens' Band there called the *Skyliners Orchestra* who feature music of the thirties and forties and who perform regularly at their centrally located City Hall. The intimacy and modest charm of these evenings has become a remarkable source of thought provoking and first time impressions for us. The band is made up entirely of musicians who for the love of this music, volunteer their time and talent at no cost. The dances occur the third Thursday of each month and there is no charge to the public except what they might choose to drop in a jar.

There are musicians representing a range of age or levels of experience and the performances are an opportunity for the public to help this sort of band strive toward their remarkable capacity to impart a larger context and reflection.

The very public venue they have chosen is an appealing and symbolic place and a growing number of listeners turn out to enjoy the evening or take advantage of the circular dance floor, which has on many occasions filled to capacity. The audience, not surprisingly, is mostly seniors, but there are usually a few of us present representing the younger generation. On one particular occasion my wife and I were very conspicuously the youngest in attendance. An elderly woman arriving late quickly ascertained the dynamic of the audience and that there were no chairs available of the vacant kind. She strode robustly over to where I sat, and stood immediately behind me. I puzzled this for a moment and then suddenly remembered my upbringing and that young people once offered their chairs to seniors. I thought that this must be like that and so offered her the convenience which she so clearly sought. She accepted it immediately, informing me as I carried out her wish to have it relocated to her preferred vantage, that she had just recently turned ninety-three! I parted with it gladly, amazed at this lady's obvious vitality and intrigued that I had landed in a social situation where some form of civil etiquette was still expected of me. This intrigue soon turned to a kind of brooding unease as I realised how narrow my life had become, so many years having passed since I had found the need of this simple intergenerational courtesy.

If you have grown up identifying primarily with the sound of amplified electric guitars, troubling away at their isolation, you cannot help at last but be taken by the simple organic intimacy of these live orchestras, reproducing those timeless standard melodies of mankind's social and romantic inclinations. The whole atmosphere offers a completely different view on the contemporary auto-verifying needs of a purely consumer or instant-gratification-based economy. A person of my generation need only to carefully hold one of these musical instruments in their hands and to examine the quality and workmanship that goes into its construction to realize that we have stepped out of our own world of cheap and disposable products and into a world of entirely different references. It is a coming into contact with a market-transcending object which exceeds our own period of planned obsolescence or blind disposable consumption. It is like discovering some hitherto unknown dimension to one's own practical expectation or explanation of community. These objects, band and orchestra instruments, do not fit easily into any category that my con- temporary culture can easily recognise and every supporting aspect of their construction speaks to some remarkable achievement of our ancestry. The materials alone, literally 'stardust from the heavens,' sifted from the very soil beneath our feet; zinc and copper to form the alloy of brass and other elements to form stainless steel; cork and organic fabrics to form gaskets and cushions and springs and rods to extend the human finger, and an unbounded human curiosity, to uncover the behaviour of a column of air confined to a tube. Nature never knew the sound of four trombones, moving so smoothly through a perfect progression, in perfect pitch, focusing the unspoken identity of an entire generation into a single timeless moment. All these wonderful instruments have found their own equivalent moments in the hands of musicians who have understood both their heritage and their medium. We owe a debt of explicit gratitude and material support that there are people who will study and perform in this deliberate act of cultivating a broader social hindsight.

After enjoying perhaps a year of these intimate concerts, a new face appeared and it became apparent that the orchestra had acquired a vocalist. As suggested before, my generation was inadvertently brought up to express a core value of strategic or reflex social insulation – we do not place ourselves into an established cultural context without some form of spatial/psychological insurance, and so, without understanding the complex tradition which was about to follow, I wondered where this man intended to 'hide'. There was no wildly cheering audience to encourage or pay for his revealing performance. This man was simply going to step up to the microphone, in a small intimate setting, and sing.

Step up to the microphone and sing was exactly what he did. As the piece of music unfolded its dignified treatment of anticipation and the vocalist patiently awaited his part, I felt, for the first time, the depth and burden of my generation's unconscious cynicism and structural callousness. As I heard his very first line give living form to my grandparents' sense of eternity, I felt like an intruder, like a spy from a different moment where hope had been squandered and innocence left to founder on the vulnerability of its own condition. I felt dishonest, unclean, and in an immediate fear of being found out. The orchestra and their new vocalist continued their piece of music unaware of the astonishing effect that they were having on my decidedly post-war contemporary disposition. As the piece of music drew to a close and resolved itself in utter reflective perfection, I knew the days were over where I could believe that I knew anything for certain or that one's social balance could be addressed by a single generational reference alone. *Skylark,* and the courageous intimacy of a living human voice, singing unconditionally, had entered my consciousness at the same moment, and I became aware that I was inheriting a richness of culture that could never be repaid. It shattered the remaining reference points of my contemporary or peer social disposition.

Our new vocalist went on to sing another song that evening and it had exactly the same effect. In the months that would lie ahead there were a total of three songs that would become imprinted on our minds as a single and deeply cherished moment. *Skylark* was the first piece he chose to sing followed by *Embraceable You* and then finally *The Nearness Of You*. We had several opportunities to hear the band and vocalist perform these three old-style romantic pieces and it never failed to strike us as an immediate discovery of almost bewildering good fortune. These songs were presented to us in a manner which supported our growing impression that time was harvesting yet a deeper significance to this music. The exercise of coming together to authentically remember a larger human experience struck me as the most current social moment I could recall recently having experienced. We went on from that day to develop a real appreciation for the role of the human voice in the orchestra setting. The vocalist did not impose himself or the lyric upon the audience or the piece, always allowing the beautiful sounds of the orchestra to draw out the very shape of the melody's words. He understood and demonstrated a balanced performance, singing only on those numbers where that particular atmosphere would seem truly enhanced by an unassuming human voice.

We always felt that these vocal pieces were precious in a sort of fragile way and so would be sure to get up for a turn or two around the dance floor. It was an impression that turned out to be sadly appropriate. This gentleman, a retired science teacher, who had understood the art and relevance of a perhaps uncharacteristically poetic reflection, had stepped forward with a personal courage to lend his voice where the silence was simply unacceptable. His vision to tackle a need where the ensuing result would bring a degree of vulnerability was perhaps the truer essence of education. He brought to our relatively youthful ears these three experiences that would challenge the inertia of our chronological location in time. Somewhere during the weeks of learning the words to a fourth piece, this retired teacher suddenly fell ill and his particular voice was lost forever. I had observed and taken note of some occasional looks of criticism on the faces of some in the audience each time this man had approached the microphone. The orchestra was subsequently obliged to return to its purely instrumental condition. No one stepped forward to challenge the silence that now hung over the whole experience[4]. It seems to me that there is both an emotional and a socially observable balance to the symmetry of human voice and orchestral instrumentation. The vocal sentiments and complex harmonies that issue out of the 1940's reveal something truly astonishing about the human condition. Apparently it takes an academic humility to attend and listen as an audience and courage for the vocalist/teacher, to believe that there will be this collective goodwill.

Our exposure to this music has released a flood of previously unheeded reality checks. It has reminded and demonstrated to us the fact that you can and will lose loved ones, sometimes in an instant. We have been struck by so many words from so many different songs that we are only now just learning how to hear. One such line is something to the effect of '...*our first hello began our last good-bye*'.

Many millions of lives and loves have come and gone in the duration of this music. We had daily been taking each other's presence largely for granted, never really embracing or appreciating that the moments of youth and good health are indeed the exception and not the rule. Our exposure to this music has brought a deeper fulfilment to our relation which we were not aware was missing. Where once we saw ourselves as infinitely unique, we now discover ourselves to be infinitely related. We are but fleeting moments in an unbroken succession of men and women seeking companionship and expression in each other's presence. It was never ours to claim ownership over. We did not invent the sexes or human companionship and so the particular couple's intimacy cannot rightly be relegated to the territory of possession – without sustaining an injury to any sense

---

4   A female teacher eventually stepped forward and she is still performing with the orchestra today which has since become a highly respected and cherished dance band

of larger human compassion. Does not each one of us represent, at the very least, the entirety of his/her manifest gender? Does not the knowledge of this hint at a reduction to those troubling antagonisms fuelled by the commercially exploited sexual distinctions? There has never been a time of such surprising mystery to our lives as since this discovery of a clearly universal element in each other.

One of our greatest pleasures has become those evenings out where there is a Big Band to dance to and people to watch. We have come up with an amusing way to predict what level of enjoyment is likely to be found at such events. It is fairly simple. We just ask ourselves, "How many of those in attendance will be seniors?" We have found, without exception, that the higher the number, the better. The explanation for this seems to boil down to experience and of course seniors have this and so you are more likely to find an evening that reflects the timeless element of life. No mature person would struggle through a lifetime of hurts, isolations and disappointments and then bring some negative aspect of that learning curve to the social celebration, it just isn't done. When seniors arrive at the dance hall, they bring with them a best behaviour, a lifetime of tested experience and a determination to enjoy every last minute of the evening's companionship. There is no sense of competitiveness or territory to defend. Just people who want and are very glad to be together.

As insightful as this rule of thumb seems to be, it suggests a rather ominous thing. At some point the secret of these pleasant social evenings will have to be verbalized and passed on to a next generation of seniors or the charm, significance and importance of these social affirmations will pass into history. It is wonderful that there are so many dance instructors ready to show us how it's done, but there is a world of difference between the structured and unrealistic expectations of what the dance schools seem to foster and what the actual, authentic and possibly disappearing social phenomenon is.

Companionship, celebrating one's own relation to history, honest thankfulness and an appreciation of the world's costly, diverse and so often tragic heritage, cannot be taught or nurtured much less remembered amid the quasi-ballroom confusion of what one senior described as *"...these pathetic store-bought dance routines"*. A simple foxtrot, enjoyed a half dozen times a year, on a crowded dance floor, will yield more lasting pleasure to more people than any mechanical routine exercised in an awkward display of contrived accomplishment or jilted rhythm. There is a rather shocking lack of simple awareness or even basic courtesy coming out of these dance schools. They seem to miss what could have been a very pleasurable opportunity. In fact, the presentation of some of this dance school curriculum seems to reflect the blanket assumption or unspoken ideal of an imagined competition, and of course, this very obvious aggression flies in the face of why mature couples find themselves gravitating naturally toward this music. More important than any repertoire of polished dance steps is an awareness of how our own mortality relates to the timeless communication and experience that this music embodies. More important than any repertoire of polished dance steps is the sensibility to realize when it is time to share the floor, with others, who have also been invited to enjoy the evening. These dances are only viable if the floor is for the most part full. The couples that you see there blending unobtrusively with each other are not captive audiences provided for the indulgent contrast of your dance school curriculum. It is they who accommodate you, not you who accommodate them. You will never match in study the grace in life their steps have both learnt and perhaps in your eyes forgotten. We have for nearly a decade been attending dances all over the southern part of our province and have never once been made to feel unwelcome by the seniors around us. Some of them, by mere statistics alone, must have been enjoying their very last dance together. Think of what this gracious hospitality means.

Just when we thought we had even this part figured out a new event took place at a local Big Band festival. A day was set aside for high school bands to come and demonstrate their skills. They were remarkable and all present enjoyed a wonderful time. There was a dance hall filled with student musicians, their parents and several groups of seniors, who were clearly delighted with the spectacle. The only group absent in disproportionate numbers was my generation, the 'off the street' thirty to sixty sort of age group. My demographic needs to be asking itself what it is we think we are accommodating by cutting back or ignoring so many of these larger context-building programs which round out our education system. Watching these students as they interact together, their fun and growing ability, their feeling of belonging and excited anticipation of bringing individual efforts together into a whole larger than the sum, I remember vividly, in myself, that same sense of excitement and growing confidence I see now in their faces. What remarkable co-operations might they go on to achieve? Was it not, at least in part, the involvement in my school's music program that protected my eroding human dignity as the purely academic/social prejudice cut away any and all effective social/economic relevance? Was it not my involvement in the school's music program that nurtured the seed of a larger sustaining human relation beyond economy?

A friend, being aware of my growing fascination for this music, remarked, *"Get with the times, you're living in the past."* Back at the harbour, I stood amongst those pieces of equipment at The Ship Builder's Memorial. It was a perfect June morning, water sparkling all around to the touch of summer's first truly warm and inviting breeze. Am I, *"...living in the past"?*

To the east, that same morning breeze was already raising the thousands of tiny ripples, which would form thousands of tiny prisms, which would bend the light so you could see directly into the water as if viewed from above. Later in the day, as the sun rose overhead, this remarkable condition would reveal numerous large shadows beneath the water's surface, placed at strategic intervals, in obvious rows. I knew from the direct recollections of a legendary local resident that these shadows were created by large piles of boulders which once served as anchoring fill for mooring cribs, which occupied a good portion of the shallow east basin.

Directly inshore from these cribs had stood a sawmill and logs were floated in from Killarney, which lay to the north at the opposite end of the bay. These 'floats' or 'rafts' of logs were secured to the cribs and this same morning sun no doubt evaporated the night's dew from their top sides as they waited silently to be drawn on to the conveyer and abruptly processed into lumber.

My legendary acquaintance, *"old Steamer C–,"* told me that if I looked I would find concrete left on the mill site from various footings critical to that operation. I looked and found them. He told me that if I looked closer, underwater, at those piles of anchoring crib fill, that I would find that some of the 'boulders' were actually bags of hardened cement, which had been cargo on a ship and had got wet, and so were put to good use regardless of the mishap. I looked with the aid of snorkel, mask and fins and found evidence of this also. Small fish were found taking good advantage of these underwater cairns. My senior companion seemed driven to pass along and point out this sort of knowledge and I found myself developing a surprisingly urgent imperative to receive it. In so far as direct interaction, this man, more than twice my corresponding age, did more to bring tangible history alive than any other single person. He was able to tell me, as we sorted through a selection of old photographs, which day of the week a 1929 picture was taken, owing to which of the

Shipyard smokestacks was captured in operation. His fascination for linking still existing phenomena to historical fact was infectious and now I cannot pass a set of steps cast into the concrete at the harbour without seeing the *Norisle,* as she sat moored to that very spot, brand new, in 1946.

Am I living in the past? On the west side of the 'spit,' or 'Heritage Drive,' as it's now called, lie the last bodies of evidence that a thriving shipbuilding industry once filled this harbour with sound and activity. *The Queens Dry Dock,* opened in 1883, and the already unbelievable *Launch Basin* now mark the silent passage of each chronological day by revealing the gentle movement of air over their unbroken surface. They built war ships here, *'Corvettes,'* and they sailed out of this very harbour, under the same sun, making the same lapping sounds as their flush riveted steel hulls eased out through the channel, past the still existing terminals and into the blue of Georgian Bay.

A modern day car passes the harbour front area at the foot of Hurontario Street, its sound system amplified to the point of an invasive absurdity. Another driver slows for a moment to verify an unfamiliar route; three more squeeze through the red light because the yellow 'should have been theirs'. At the mouth of the harbour, the Corvette-class *H.M.C.S. Collingwood's* engine-room telegraph signals "SLOW AHEAD." Another group of young men are cast into roles from which there will be no escape.

Discouraged by the seemingly insurmountable degree of neurological isolation that separates man I wander back toward where my own vehicle waits. Inadvertently, I have left a tape playing, the now familiar strains of a favourite wartime song imparting a striking and urgent need for the resolution of man's imagined alienation. Fifty physical years separate my senior companion and I. The inevitable happens. Alone, I retrace the steps of that fleeting relationship and consider the meaning of these brand new memories.

These wartime songs are the sound of the past pleading with the future. In countless cases these melodies must represent the last moments of relief, reflection and relatively pleasant social interaction experienced by those whose passing forever scars the integrity of humankind's consciousness. How many people enjoyed these very sounds, perhaps even these very recordings, only hours or even moments before this reckoning with history tore them from our embrace. This parting of and in such fashion has injured eternity and this music leads me effortlessly to that mortal edge. I did not enter this world or begin to think as an adult for decades to come yet this music haunts me like the personal memories of a witness to some ghastly crime, and the fact of it, imparts an implication of stewardship that challenges the founding assumption of my generation. Countless legions of people, unspeakable numbers, not even half my present age, perished in these hellish outcomes of attempted sequential validation. And here am I at forty years old, with all these opportunities at my disposal, still not feeling grown up.

The situation forces the disturbing question, *'When do I become an adult; when do I feel grown up'?* If I achieve all these little consumer game pieces that society sets out, does that make me an adult? If I achieve an imagined personal security and personal satisfaction without regard for the big picture, does that make me an adult? If I cling to a particular belief system, proclaiming its supreme authority over all other belief systems, does that – make me an adult? If I cling to a so-called observable fact, as if I alone had achieved perfect social objectivity, does that make me an adult? If I persist and pursue the prevailing neuro-chemical concept of absolute individuality, to the point of tangible or outward manifest contention, does this make me an adult, a complete human being? If I were to pursue all of these things and find accomplices to verify the shape and apparent legitimacy of that pursuit, does this equal the net worth of all those souls cast historically into the abyss of unspeakable violence? Have

I, through any act of simple 'marketplace consumption,' earned the right or adult integrity to question or articulate what the nature of a 'freedom,' bought through such incomprehensible suffering and loss of life, might look like?

What would happen if a person reached the end of their effort to manifest as an individual amongst individuals? What would happen if a person just simply called society's bluff – *'there is no 'absolute neurological individual,' only a web of endless interdependent relationship and the opportunity to confound or embrace that kinship'*. Would this be the act of a child – or the act of an adult? I do not challenge the indisputable suffering of the particular human being, but rather the ambiguity of the assumption which negates the compassion I should naturally have felt. Why are we, as particular 'individual persons,' unable to relate to each other's 'personal plight'?

During the war years, your generation gained first hand personal experience of what will happen when global populations indulge in divisive social/sequential enterprises. There was never any pressing political imperative to articulate it with philosophically or culturally transcending language, because you already knew the outcome. Your generation has this unspoken burned-by-experience self-restraint. Your generation has practised its remedial suspension of wholesale explicit cultural/political ambition. It has been a good and necessary step, but the issue has yet to be strategically or perhaps more accurately, legally dealt with. The divisive chronological aspect of thought, as manifest through time, in abstract states of ambiguous constitutional language, has of course remained; and in the absence of any democratically successful attempts to legally or morally state the 'physical parameters' of 'thought itself,' or perhaps even the subsequently flawed 'thought-projected' larger strategy of 'public education' – beyond contemporary social/economic policy – has of course mutated into this multitude of suicidal corporate and/or corporate/individual counter-environmental, counter-cultural empires. The ball has been resoundingly dropped by more than just one generation. The problem has never been challenged to full social articulate clarity, and so we are, still, despite unspeakable losses of life, vulnerable.

My generation, through its lack of a mutually affirming socio-academic process, drifts precariously close to a disposition looking increasingly similar to a 'pre-war over-simplification.' The knee-jerk emotional withdrawal all the way back to super simplistic econo-culture or mono-specific identifications has not been recognised for the global disaster it most certainly guarantees. My generation does not have your burned-by-experience insight at either end of the scale so it becomes inevitable that we must and will most surely achieve a crystal clear articulation of what constitutes both an 'appropriate' and an 'inappropriate' application of mechanically sequential neurological activity. We must learn, very quickly, how to defuse the division of our signature based, locality oriented thought process, and illustrate both our desire and consensus to achieve an authentic social adulthood through a conscious global/universal identification. Mankind is more than the prejudicial or fleeting order in which childlike or neurologically innocent impressions strike him.

My generation needs this last gift from a generation that can hardly be asked to give again. We need you to understand that we cannot embrace the culturally coloured and often over-simplified presentation of sacrifice as it so commonly manifests. We need to know exactly what it is that history has bought and paid for through each and every one of these inexcusable and unspeakable sequential deaths. Not more of the same, surely? History is the blood of human consciousness, the measure of how far we have compromised our deeper intelligence. We need you to back this up, to acknowledge the darker social implication of each and every consequent death. You must allow us the contemporary relevance of questioning all institutions and sub-sequent social dis-integrations which lead to division and ultimately violence. You cannot expect us to believe that there is no neurological link. When we are asked to think about the sacrifices that were made on our behalf, but are not allowed to consider the underlying aspect of our broader consequential existence, which obviously precipitates these darkest moments, you are asking us to endorse the un-endorsable. We know that an exclusive belief in any one specific thing is an observable precursor to conflict. This is the one rock solid conviction of my generation and it is the essence of the condition that is dividing us from our past. Mine is the generation, which must through inescapable necessity, question the very medium out of which springs both the individual civilian and his conflict prone group, nation or religious state. Clearly we are collapsing under the weight of this logical progression from your post-war social renunciation experiment.

I listen to this music of the war years because I want to understand the epic pain of your generation's loss. But I cannot effectively open that personal floodgate unless you acknowledge, even in the tiniest way, the unprecedented position of my generation's burden of judgement. History will judge through the weakest link in a chain of collective integrity. We cannot allow ourselves to grieve openly for that which has yet to be honestly clarified, lest it become an ambiguous endorsement of our unspeakable past. We are asking you to forgive our appearance of indifference, to have faith in us, and to look for ways to understand and recognise the awkward development of our very sincere respect and deep sense of duty toward your generation.

In the entreaty of Flanders Fields, we find the delicate core of our single greatest civil-inheritance at its greatest risk. The memory and meaning of sacrifice has been left perilously unclear. We must revisit the poem, or become the generation who severed history for want of an honest discussion.

Beyond Time

I sat on a warm summer's afternoon at beautiful Sunset Point on Georgian Bay. I had brought with me a comfortable chair, a lunch and a thermos of hot water to make tea. It was a day and location which did in fact lead you to believe that the world had noted history and had accordingly made its requisite adjustments as per region, culture and local manifestation of those larger insights. Trees had been planted and time had affirmed the thought; the green of maturing cedars and pines against the blue of endless sky against the sound of ceaseless waves against the surface of ancient shale, had created in me, exactly the effect the gardener envisioned. On this particular day I was two hours just taking it all in. Eventually I got around to lunch and immediately after began amending a list of jobs and errands.

In a short while, I was approached by an individual who mistook my notepad and thoughtful gaze to the horizon as the characteristic and demeanour of an artist. He was visibly disappointed to learn that I was in fact troubling over the details of a shopping list. A conversation ensued and I learnt that my visitor was an art student from a university in Toronto and that soon he would be leaving for Paris to study sculpture. He explained that he found his study in oil unfulfilling and that what he needed was to work in the three dimensions of sculpting to fully express his creative potential.

Finding that I was either unable, unwilling or uncomfortable commenting on his search for a suitable outlet of self-expression, he moved on to the subject of politics and social studies. Apparently I used the wrong wording when I communicated that I thought there could be difficulty lying ahead for all of us and this he mistook for an invitation to air some very troubling views. At about this time another man happened along and, recognising the characteristic and essential demeanour of a speech about to transgress the boundaries of acceptable, he sat himself down to enjoy the encounter.

This second man was older. His attire and personal carriage seemed to suggest a long-time successful businessman. I felt relief at his approach because I was certain that his age and experience would bring a moderating element to the situation. I felt sure that his timely arrival would temper the 'artist's' rhetoric and perhaps the encounter could be redirected before something truly unfortunate was said.

As they spoke, it became painfully clear that they were actually in agreement on all aspects of the subject. The problem, apparently, was that there were *"too many people in the world"* and *"too many third world producers undercutting the first world economies."* Bolstered by this second and eagerly interactive member of his audience the 'artist' intensified the nature of his rhetoric and of course uttered the unthinkable. *"...We need another war!"* [5]

One must try to envision the situation. The 'artist,' standing erect, feet planted firmly apart, striking ever such an authoritative pose. The somewhat ageing 'businessman,' availing himself of the Rotary Club park bench in a natural way and I, reclining on the recycled lounge chair I had brought along, cup of tea in one hand, half-compiled shopping/to-do list in the other. I had been coming to this very spot for years bringing my chair, my lunch and a modest resolve to be a reasonable human being. As an adolescent, I had been forced into hard and unpopular decisions based in part on that simple resolve, decisions which had haunted me to this very day. As the 'artist' uttered his unthinkable words in this blessed, fortunate and peaceful place, the repercussion of those past decisions transformed themselves into a first real inclination of a personal or perhaps tangible adult-

---

5   This encounter and original manuscript predate the events of 911.

hood. I had always felt a degree of intimidation in the presence of those whose nature fit so easily with the status quo, their unconscious social/self-righteous confidence apparently being impenetrable from the outside. As his words sunk in the obscene irony of the situation solidified itself and I felt the power of these two individuals to threaten me begin to dissolve. I determined that on this day I would no longer remain silent.

I must have shifted in my chair or given some indication of this spontaneous resolve because my two visitors suspended their mutual affirmations and fell silent. I did not know how but I was going to counter their conversation and so was glad of the awkward moment to force my involvement. In my head, I desperately ran the basis of a still vague response through its logical progression. Like the last and near hopeless deployment of a life ring upon a dark sea, I threw the thought into action even before the details had made themselves clear. After what must have struck them as an intellectual eternity, I addressed myself to the 'artist.' "Let me be sure that I understand you." "You are saying that *we need another war to improve things!*" The 'artist' responded, "yes – I am!"

We should review at this juncture the projected and apparent backgrounds of the participants in this discussion. The 'artist,' as he told me, was studying at a Toronto university. He mentioned having obtained other degrees but that art was now his passion. The 'businessman,' although not necessarily so, could also have held university or other such degrees. Whatever his background and training was, he gave every indication of having achieved enough experience and position to get on top of and stay on top of some enterprise. Whatever their specific details were, they both clearly occupied the territory of contemporary social, political and economic currency. Of the three of us, I would have been, beyond anyone's question, the least relevant by society's measure. As is the usual in such situations, I did not explicitly draw attention to this detail of my background.

After having established beyond doubt that the 'artist' felt that we needed *'a war to improve things'* I addressed myself to the 'business-man.' *"Do you agree that we need a war to improve things?"* The 'businessman,' having had more time to refine his social manner at least knew that his view was not something to be indiscriminately proud of. After an awkward moment of reflection, and for me, surprising personal honesty, he quietly affirmed, *"yes!"* I turned to the 'artist.' *"So you are saying that the children in one country must die – so that the children in another country can live in comfort!"* The 'artist' responded, *"Yes – I am!"* I turned to the 'businessman.' *"Do you agree?"* (Hesitation) *"– Yes!"* I re-addressed myself to the 'artist.' *"So you are saying that the children on one side of the street must die – so that the children on the other side of the street can live in comfort.* The 'artist' responded, *"Yes; – I am!"* I turned to the 'businessman,' *"Do you agree?"* (Growing hesitation) *"– Yes!"* I returned to the 'artist,' *"So you are saying that my child must die – so that your child can live in comfort!"* The 'artist' hesitated only a second then responded, *"Yes – I guess I am!"* and the tone of his voice offered no hint of apology. The absurdity of the encounter left us in silence. To defuse the confrontation I at last confided that I did not myself actually have children.

All of a sudden time was *'getting on'* and my two visitors excused themselves departing in opposite directions. I sat in utter disbelief at the ridiculous nature of the confrontation. Gradually, in tiny manageable portions, it dawned on me that I had not wasted my life after all. Here were two men, borne on a summer's breeze, inwardly steeped in society's honoured institutions, enjoying both the economic and/ or social currency of living in one of the world's most fortunate countries, and yet, still, inciting acts of the most unspeakable and profound ignorance. And here was I, the 'never amount to anything high school dropout,' with a predictably diminished social/economic currency, with no real, fancied or gainful stake in this outward society, yet still, willing to defend the ideals of those same honoured institutions.

I could not and still cannot think of words for it. It is the most obscene turn of social/cultural events. How could all the sacrifice and suffering have come to this? All of those countless people who died unspeakable deaths, trying to resolve or being caught in the resolution of man's historic alienation. The majority of us are, by virtue of our continued silence on this blatant academic hypocrisy, a disgrace to the highly and technologically documented history that is our collective humankind. We are moving too fast, in too many directions, with no clearly defined instrument of consciousness. If the possession of a 'self' means adopting and defending a concept of time so flimsy and ambiguous that only the fashionable appetites of a neuro-consumer/commerce hold sway, then I want no part of it.

There was a period, before this surprising encounter with our parents' music, when our personal economic situation was even less tenable than today. Someone kindly allowed us the use of a tiny isolated cottage in exchange for repairs and upkeep and we stayed there quite a number of years. Our childhood and adolescent contemporaries had long since moved on to well paying jobs and trendy careers and with that had quite naturally embraced the preoccupied indifference which seems so inseparable from an apparently 'healthy economic activity'. We lived in this tiny cottage tucked into the woods with no electricity or running water. We carried in supplies as needed and lit our evenings with oil lamps and candles. In the winter, we heated with wood and in those long evenings, time for reflection was very much indeed our personal wealth. Our social and philosophic isolation grew in a direct proportion to that activity and soon the music that we had grown up with became like salt in an open wound. We turned off our little radio, removed its batteries and spent our evenings reading or chatting about the direction of our lives or sitting quietly by the fire in thoughtful silence.

In the summer the wind did 'gust through the forest canopy and sound like an unseen ocean breaking on an unseen shore'. In the winter, 'silent nights would be measured by frost splitting the tree trunks.' There were 'creatures and phenomena for every season' and we did come to know a lot of them. There was a particular species of beetle, local to us, which had its observable moment in the spring. They could be found at night, on the forest floor, 'plying their trade beneath last year's blanket of discarded leaves.' They were notable for an interesting characteristic. They could be startled when their activities were interrupted by heavy footsteps. If you came down the trail quietly and then stamped your feet, you could hear them recoil into defensive or evasive positions, the rustling sound coming from every direction as they scrambled for cover. For such a tiny creature, they had a remarkable capacity for memory and would only allow themselves to be startled once per fifteen-minute encounter.

We lived this way a total of eight years, contemplating and enjoying the sights and sounds around us. Remarkable though it was, we also found that 'heaven and society could not be accepted under such terms'. We dusted off our little radio, connected it to a battery and began searching the dial. Station after station was broadcasting the same thumping contemporary affirmation that only affirmed our sense of isolation. We performed this exercise repeatedly with no clear idea of what we sought, each time returning the radio to its mute place on the shelf.

One evening while performing this ritual, we came across a program celebrating the music of the Big Band era. I launched into a supposedly learned commentary on what this music was about, identifying and describing which instruments made what sounds and, mechanically, how it was accomplished. Having played in the high-school band, I had come away thinking I knew it all.

Eventually my capacity to profess any kind of intelligence on the matter gave way to the silent realisation that I knew nothing about this music. I knew nothing about the people who had performed it, the people who continued to enjoy it, or of the real circumstances under which it was written, or why, for that matter, its continued existence should seem so suddenly bursting with significance. Hour after hour we listened as melodies were offered up in the most casual presentation, as if the whole senior population had been quietly observing this moment. A surprising number of the melodies were known to us, a couple with shocking intimacy. We could not reconcile the apparent previous knowledge of these melodies with the dramatically new and liberating way in which they seemed to strike us. Eventually the show's host wound the program down toward a finish and bid his listeners good night, pointing out that the program could be heard each week during the same time slot. He repeated his farewell greeting and faded in a piece of music whose familiarity to and impact upon us could not have been anticipated. The piece of music unfolded itself with a dignified resignation that left our thoughts reeling to fill in the gaps of our understanding before the melody or program would end. I was desperate to understand it but could not. The piece of music ended, the evening ended, and the broadcaster returned to its contemporary format. Brutally wrenched from one solitude to another I bolted from my chair to disconnect the radio and preserve the moment. We sat once more in silence. Our candle had exhausted itself an hour earlier. We did not speak. We had possessed no previous knowledge or experience of conscious change, it usually being a gradual thing, an unconscious thing, but the radio program had altered our perception of identity within a single evening. We sat in silence – a dark and appalling silence. It was a silence in which the magnitude of man's isolation was made both brutally and starkly obvious. We were conscious for the first time of how profoundly unhappy we had been. Not with each other or the choices we had made, but with the lack of an acceptable or accessible way to think about or view our true relation to a larger society. Gradually this appalling emptiness gave way to the unpredictable rhythm of the sound that the wind makes, gently rising and falling amongst the trees. There was no other sound. Only this ceaseless variation of atmosphere interacting with its earth, sounding exactly as it had eons before mankind uttered his first word. I did not sleep that night, obsessed with the need to contrast the memory of the impression of the music I had just heard with the ageless singing of the wind in this timeless succession of trees. It had been my first inclination of what a useful maturity might feel like. In the years that would follow, the sound of this single program filled our tiny cottage with a warmth and hope of a larger society unlike anything we had previously imagined. It caused a dramatic reassessment of all our social assumptions and ushered in by far the most productive period of growth and reflection in our lives.

Always, and forever, it seems, I am drawn back to this harbour. First to the Shipbuilders' Memorial, to lay a hand on the old dry-dock steam engine and then across the promenade to look at the shear-leg footings, the crane which during the war years hoisted the 'Scotch boilers' aboard the Corvettes as they lay moored to this very dock. After a quick look at the names on the memorial stone I turn to look upon the Dry-Dock and Launch Basins themselves. Soon this area will be developed into a waterfront housing and retail centre and public access by both land and sea to these historic Great-Lake docks has apparently been promised.

How will the drama and history of this modest site be communicated to the new residents and future visitors? How will the existing
community explain that the empty Grain Terminals to the north
capture their heritage as would a silent family portrait rendered on a
canvas as big as the sky. These naturalized concrete pillars are worthy
of any art gallery anywhere. Built in 1929, this deliberately preserved
rail and shipping link has become a highly cherished visual landmark
and has been a welcome beacon for all manner of past/present land
based and marine activity on south-Georgian and Nottawasaga Bay
waters. Through its presence and central waterfront location, the
terminal silos themselves have become the single most significant
and lasting monument to Collingwood's undeniable contribution to
Canadian Great Lakes Shipping and with their classic architecture and
aesthetically pleasing proportions, they have succeeded in capturing
early-to-mid twentieth century engineering and shipping aspirations
with a surprising and I suspect wholly unforeseen dignity.

How shall we make ourselves remember that these ripples on
our harbour, reach out unbroken through time, to touch the very
fact of every human experience? Young men sailed out of this small
shipbuilding port to meet a war that was not supposed to happen.
Through the physical and time embracing nature of the water, I
touch the very steel of their ships as they fade on the horizon. In the
summer afternoons, I bathe in the clear waters off Sunset Point, east
of the Terminals, to feel the inescapable truth of it. Though the shale
is slippery and the zebra mussels can nick your feet and there can be
dangerous currents if the wind and waves should rise, the overriding
sensation remains one of healing and renewal and I attribute this to
the nearby proximity of such elegant and historic municipal assets.

Always it is the ripples, too many for any one brain to grasp. Is
it not important to at least acknowledge that the majority of human
intelligence never makes it past the first editor? How will I know if
I have been honest, where I have been trained to think like a wave

instead of the sea? Can they ever actually be separated and who should I trust to suggest whether it is love or self-interest, and who among us should be invited to 'participate in that consensus' needed to address whether it could ever have been sustainable to push the division that far? Two percent of the actual 'human being' might be attributed to the specific body, yet the other ninety-eight percent of innocent vulnerability goes unattended because the former cannot bring its greedy bearing to focus on the larger question.

Back at the harbour, you can continue north/west from the Shipbuilder's Memorial to see how the perspective of the Terminals changes with every footstep. Past the Yacht Club and Watts Skiff building, where they are celebrating the town's very first industry by preserving a working replica of the double-ended wooden fishing boats that once plied these waters. And if you look east across the shallow natural basin, toward Sunset Point, you can actually make out the ridge of shale just below the sparkling surface, which once offered protection from the open water to the earliest people of the region and by extension, held out the promise of the vibrant and creative shipbuilding industry that was to follow.

At the tip of Heritage Drive, north of the Terminals, is a good view north and west over the open water. To the western horizon Collingwood's Nottawasaga Lighthouse warns sailors of that same ridge-formation that created the safe-harbour itself. Dating to the very year of the town's incorporation, the presence of this Imperial Lighthouse has been woven inextricably into the consciousness of the entire region and it speaks volumes to the unique challenges and triumphs of Great Lakes marine navigation.

At the terminus of Heritage Drive is a large cast-iron ship's propeller, lying in a garden of rock and pebble looking exactly the way it looked, underwater, where it lay undetected for perhaps a hundred years. No one is left who can remember which ship it was that strayed out of the channel and so sheered off its main-shaft where it entered the hub of this impressive casting. All of the ships are gone now and the silent harbour has become like a port in waiting, looking to see which way the wind might blow or what new product might be shipped to an unknown market. Could there not be some sort of new vessel, that might navigate by the points of a compass responding to a universal heading and having for its keel a clear and concise understanding of precisely what human thought is? Has the world really found any true or lasting happiness solely through the tangible assets hoisted aboard a ship? Have we stopped to consider how much displacement it will require, to float a universally neglected human consciousness?

They launched massive ships here into a basin of just fifteen feet of water. To those of us who never saw it done, it remains an unequivocal impossibility, yet you can see it unfold on film at the town's nearby museum. How is one to grasp the scope and scale of what was physically accomplished in so little space? I like to compare the dimensions of these locally built vessels to the community's nearby historic water tower. Located just inland from the harbour this municipal tower provides a convenient measure to size up the fabrication and launching of those massive ships. The tower itself can be seen clearly from the harbour's Heritage Drive or from several locations along the connecting bike and walking trail. The ships were said to have been five or more stories high as they rested on the launch way, which means that if one were lying on dry land at the foot of the water tower, its deck railing would have reached approximately half way to the top of the tower. If one of these ships had been stood on end, it would itself have dwarfed the municipal structure by almost five times! The imagery seems logistically inconceivable yet the specifications and events are documented fact.

Looking inland toward the water tower, you are struck by its classic 1940s 'Art Deco' style. I am not sure if that is the right categoriza-

tion to use but as you take the fifteen to twenty minute stroll down
the promenade toward it, you are struck by the bold and functional
use of heavy steel support pillars and gracefully fabricated 'I-beam'
components. When filled to capacity, the elegant structure supports
some 2,500 tons of water. I was lucky enough to notice the historic
and engineering features of this tower while two key figures in its
construction were still alive. One of the gentlemen was employed
directly by the town and he was responsible for the upgrading and
maintenance of water utilities. He was able to tell me about supply
and pressure problems in the 1950s and of an undersized and poorly
located fresh-water intake in the Bay itself. The other gentleman was
employed by the company that had originally built the tower and
who were subsequently contracted to disassemble and relocate the
massive structure to its new home in Collingwood. Both men spoke
with obvious pride about their roles in the purchase and relocation of
this historic landmark, and now, subsequently, I cannot visit a small
town anywhere without going to see what type of classic water tower
might still be quietly serving their needs.

The gentleman whose employer had built the structure described
how the massive support beams located under the reservoir and
radiating out from the 'center riser,' and the slightly raised centre-
point to the top of the tank itself, had given birth to that class of
towers becoming known as 'Radial Cone' in design. To appreciate
a manufactured structure like this it is necessary to approach it on
foot, to give the brain time to process the scale of the unfolding
visual perspective. I drove by this tower for years without the slightest
thought to its presence, yet approaching it on foot, I am impressed by
the bold and visionary accomplishment. If you break the structure
down into its component parts, that part which contains the water and
that part which supports it high off the ground, you can begin to see
the design logic in all its splendour. There are beautiful curves formed
right into the underside steel-plate of the reservoir and these relate

to transforming those downward forces into tensile forces, which are more easily dealt with that way. There is an oversized *'centre riser,'* which apart from bearing much of the combined weight of the structure's water and steel, ensures that in cold winter climates there is no risk of freezing. When all these immutable physics and engineering expediencies are appreciated the tower seems to revert to or take on a decidedly organic appearance, looking like a giant dewdrop or bud of crystal-clear water supported atop some sort of tree or plant-like stems. A beautifully spiralled staircase only adds to this impression of an elegant and art-like sculpture born out of and in keeping with its original affinity to nature.

The walk from the harbour to consider the size of those ships compared to this tower is not the last of your rewards. On this very same site is the town's oldest recreation facility and it holds the distinction of symbolising all the diverse things that a hometown community might offer to its citizens over the course of many generations. Built in 1909 to fulfill a variety of social/political aspirations, the building's architectural lines appear to have been drawn from the British-influenced armouries of the day. Although military training was an important part of the structure's original function, it also served as the community's Exhibition Building. With a natural ice surface during the winter months, hockey kept the building in regular use through the cold season. Every manner of social activity requiring a large open building kept the community returning decade after decade. In 1949, with the opening of a new downtown arena, hockey games ceased to be played there. With the building now empty in the winter months, the local Curling Club moved in and the preservation of this remarkable building might be attributed directly to their reliable tenancy.

In conversation with townsfolk over the historic role of this building, I was intrigued to notice the differing titles attributed to it. Old *'Steamer C—,'* approaching ninety at the time, had always referred to it as "The Drill Shed," owing to the building's service as an armoury. Other residents in the seventy to eighty year range had referred to it as the "Exhibition Building" or the "Old Hockey Arena". The rest of the younger population just call it the "Curling Club". The gentleman who thought of the building as the "Drill Shed" spoke of playing as a child in the WW1 training trenches. He spoke of the soldiers who had carved their names in the back wall of the building and I was lucky enough to find several of them, one dating to 1917. I was told of track and field days, baseball games, horse races and army cadets. I was told of the "Kiltie Band" marching through the downtown core to arrive at the Exhibition Building's band shell to play for yet another hour or more. I have seen photos of young men in military training with fixed bayonets and a scene where steam tractors are lined up like cars on a modern-day sales lot. I was told of a cold winter day when too many spectators leaned on the railing at a hockey game and it gave way spilling the fans out onto the ice surface like a line of frozen dominos. As relative newcomers to the region, my wife and I had never quite known how to refer to the old building and half in jest, we began calling it *'The Century Palace,'* in honour of those agricultural buildings of an earlier period, referred to as *'Crystal Palaces'*.

As we stood last year in a queue waiting to enter the building for a summer concert and dance, my wife and I were drawn into a conversation with three couples who had traveled from Toronto to enjoy the event. The first thing that had captured their attention was the presence of that beautiful 1940s water tower, which looks directly out over the main building and adjoining grounds. We talked about where the tower had originally come from and why that region had later offered it for sale so many years ago. We talked about the other municipalities who still retain such classic landmarks and of one community about two hours away, which has a tower that dates even further back to the 1930s. After dealing with the tower their attention turned to the historic building which we were about to enter. As I listened to their thoughts about its dated architecture, the upper course of seven arched windows and the two matching chimneys and to their surprise that a small town facility such as this could actually survive through into the twenty-first century, I thought about that title we had privately attached to it.

Drawn from all over the province and beyond the large crowd of visitors filed into the building and were treated to an evening where three different vocal musicians sequentially profiled that part of an American pop star's life which corresponded to their own biological years. Having been listening to and enjoying the Jazz Standards and Big Band music normally associated with the war years, I was not a particularly big fan of the music style being celebrated that evening. But the event did have the surprising effect of removing an impediment to my appreciation and respect for those other musical styles which evolved out of the twentieth century. After enjoying an evening where some eight hundred people had transformed the historic building into a huge 1950s dance hall, I was struck by how superficial my own media-generated impression of the annual event had been. There were many more things going on here than a simple nostalgic look into the past. While the crowd behind me looked forward to the stage, I turned to look back into their faces and the expressions that I saw there spoke of a deeply inward personal reflection and of a joy of connecting outwardly with each other, through the public affirmation of our own sequential vulnerabilities, triumphs and inevitable tragedies. Through the touchstone of an all too common and clearly complicit human frailty, in the person of the pop star being examined, this crowd was connecting not only with the hopes and aspirations of their own generation, but also with the hopes and aspirations of the vulnerable human condition in every direction. It may have been plainly obvious to those well over fifty, but it was a startling revelation to me, to make the logical connection that apart from the new 'rock & roll' beat associated with his music, Mr. Presley was, vocally speaking, first and foremost, a crooner, perhaps the last commercially successful one and as such a missing tangible link between my own generation of explicit and isolating individuality and my parents' and grandparents' era of a larger yet equally vulnerable social/political connection. I thought he was a 'rock star'. The degree of critical separation diminishes with every passing day.

What stands in the way of a world reaching out to embrace its own vulnerability? Why shouldn't I see my own generation's struggle to find its place as an extension of that single continuous thread of all human aspiration? Is it intelligence itself, that divides us, or space, generated through the product of unconscious thought? As the crowd dispersed into the night, I glanced back to imagine how this building might have looked on a similar night, nearly one hundred years ago. Once again, the building had provided a silent expression of its original mandate – to bring together and serve a larger community. From the 'century palace' and alongside the steel pillars of the 1940s water tower, we walked down the Memory Lane Trail toward the harbour. It was too nice a night to go in just yet. Past The Station and along the promenade we walked amid the shimmering lights of the harbour, until we arrived at The Ship Builder's Memorial. It was here that we had met the Merchant Marine sailor as he had stood immersed deep within his own thoughts – I remember so well the astonished surprise on his face as he realised that we were listening to his period of music by a very deliberate and personal choice. Neither of us wanted the magic of the evening to end just yet so we continued on past the Terminals and stood for a half hour under the star filled night sky, watching the steady and reassuring signal of the Nottawasaga Light. I forced myself to conjure up the image of the *H.M.C.S. Collingwood* and her crew of young seamen, as they might have looked stowing the lines and getting underway toward the mouth of the harbour. Off their starboard bow would be Woodland Beach and its still (privately) operating dance hall, which holds four or five events a year. Built in 1932, we have twice enjoyed there the sounds of a modern-day *Music Makers*. East and a little south from that venue is Orr Lake, with its original 1929 dance floor, *"...polished smooth as glass"* and their summertime resident four piece band *"North of Fifty,"* still providing a monthly blend of old country favourites, square dances and a sprinkling of Wartime Jazz Standards. This band is said to have a direct lineage to a band called the *Blue Marines,* who until the outbreak of World War 2, performed here in Collingwood at a small dance pavilion nestled in the cedars at Sunset Point. Off *H.M.C.S. Collingwood's* port bow would be the towns of Thornbury and Clarksburg, where today's *Georgian Sound Big Band* hosts its annual festival and various other dances throughout the year. I know that the older generation feels that we are letting this whole thing slip away, that we are not rising to meet the critical challenges of our time as you did in yours. But this is not entirely fair. With the implication and utterly irrevocable nature of all that the twentieth century has set in motion, we must get this right, for all peoples, with the very first words we speak. Goodbye Father. Of course I love you.

Literary/Philosophical Influences:

H.D. Thoreau   *Walden*
                      Civil Disobedience

J. Krishnamurti   *The Awakening of Intelligence*

D. Suzuki   *Metamorphosis*

Biographic Note

Born in Canada in 1959 to British parents, the author found traditional education unaccommodating to his psychological reality and subsequently dropped out of school at age sixteen. Inspired by the 1985 CBC television series *"A PLANET FOR THE TAKING"* with David Suzuki, the author initiated direct communications with provincial education authorities toward the development of a clearer explanation as to why he, as an ageing high school dropout, had found it necessary to reject the assumptions underpinning formal education. Although made to feel welcome in that 1990-91 overture, education authorities were unable to identify an 'authorized process' or 'vehicle' through which the former high school dropout could participate in meaningful discussion. In 1994, the author made a significant written submission to the subsequent Ontario Royal Commission on Learning, on the understanding that a central purpose of the Commission's work was to *'provide a forum* (authorized process) *for all stakeholders to participate'*. When the Commission's extensive findings were published, the only possible or remotely relevant trace of the author's topically legitimate submission were the categorical and ambiguous words, *'profound questions had been raised'*. Realizing that his government's commission had effectively negated, silenced and withdrawn the 'Charter Status' of his peer community's 'non-academic citizenship,' as 'stakeholders in the issue,' the unschooled participant set about developing the communication skills he would need, no matter how rustic, to challenge the established mythology-of-purpose in education.

Printed in the United States
By Bookmasters